WRITER'S GUIDE

History

HENRY J. STEFFENS

MARY JANE DICKERSON

with TOBY FULWILER
in Chapter 2

ARTHUR W. BIDDLE, *General Editor*
all of University of Vermont

D. C. HEATH AND COMPANY
Lexington, Massachusetts *Toronto*

Published simultaneously in Canada.

Printed in the United States of America.

International Standard Book Number: 0-669-12002-2

Library of Congress Catalog Card Number: 86-82753

Preface

> Writing is, after all an act — something that has to be done; and it is better to approach the teaching of it from the point of view of the creative processes rather than from the point of view of the created product, from the point of view of the doer rather than from the point of view of the thing done.
>
> Carl L. Becker, *Detachment and the Writing of History*

The best way to learn history is by writing it — that's the principle behind this book. *Writer's Guide: History* applies current writing theory to the special needs of this rewarding discipline. Historian Carl Becker's words about writing history as a creative process for the writer (and reader) describe what this book is about. The result is a powerful aid for history students at every level.

TO THE STUDENT

Whether you are a committed history major or an engineer taking an elective, whether you are enrolled in your first history course or your final seminar, if you want to understand this challenging field, *Writer's Guide* is meant for you. This book shows you how to handle important historical concepts, explains why historical interpretation remains an ongoing process (and teaches you how to distinguish among varieties of evidence), and even demystifies the research essay. You'll find help with all your writing needs in history.

TO THE INSTRUCTOR

Written by a historian and a writing specialist, *Writer's Guide: History* offers a variety of resources adaptable to virtually any course in your curriculum. Introductory students might find the first three or four chapters most valuable, leading up to a short book review, a transcribed piece of oral history, or more ambitiously, an annotated bibliography and a short essay written from a primary source. These same chapters would also prove useful for intermediate level students, but their major piece of writing might be a bibliographic essay or the short scholarly article, as explained in Chapters 5 and 6. Advanced students might propose a research project and write an extensively researched essay on their findings. Alternatively, they might prepare bibliographic essays on primary source materials in the campus library or nearby museums. Every student required to do library work will find that the chapter on library research and materials goes beyond the usual introductions. Keeping a journal (as explained in Chapter 2) seems to bring out the best in just about every student from freshman to graduate. Finally, concise guides to usage and punctuation provide handy reference aids.

Each chapter of *Writer's Guide* is designed to be self-instructional. Although the value of many assignments would be enhanced by class discussion, students can use this book independently. The purpose of several chapters is to guide the reader/writer through the steps of researching and writing a variety of papers. In the chapter on the short scholarly paper, for example, the reader learns how to select a topic from interests, then how to focus and substantiate that topic, and finally how to draw inferences and conclusions from that material. Each step culminates in a piece of writing, each piece of writing leads to the next, until the student has produced a finished essay. Undoubtedly, some instructors will simply assign a chapter as a means of assigning a paper. However you choose to use this book, we believe that it will improve your students' understanding of history, not just their writing ability.

Acknowledgments

Our special thanks go to two members of the Reference Department in the Bailey/Howe Library at the University of Vermont. Nancy Crane helped locate reference sources and Linda MacDonald provided very specific help with computer search information. We are also indebted to our students and our colleagues — especially students Patricia Tursi, Brian Cote, James Salengo, David Jamieson, and Eva-Marie Goy; and colleagues Marshall True, Littleton Long, Virginia Clark, Lynne Bond, Anthony Magistrale, Daniel Bean, Kenneth Holland, and Arthur Biddle.

Contents

[1] Writing to Learn History

PREVIEW: *The main way we learn history is to examine the available written records and artifacts from the past and interpret them by reading and writing about them. This chapter examines some basic principles for all kinds of writing and all fields of study with special attention to writing and learning history.*

WHAT IS HISTORY?

History is the sum total of past human actions: everything human beings have done, all their actions, and even their inactions. History resembles nature in that we believe both exist, but our real fascination lies in studying and learning about them. This study of history — or doing history — is usually what we mean when we say "history."

The only way we can do history is to examine the available written records and artifacts from the past and write about them. For example, studying the meticulous register of inquisition kept by the Bishop of Permiers enabled French historian Emmanuel Le Roy Ladurie to recreate life in a fourteenth-century French village in his book *Montaillou*. In another example, American historian Robert Myers edited letters written by a Georgia family before, during, and after the American Civil War in *Children of Pride*. The Jones family letters reveal many facets of daily life and subtle nuances in attitudes toward "the cause" and toward slavery. In addition to documents, much of what we know of the ancient world depends on the many artifacts uncovered through the years such as the discoveries Schliemann made about Troy and Agamemnon's buried treasure. These artifacts help historians by providing a context for the written inscriptions and records they examine.

WHY WRITE HISTORY?

Doing history always means writing history because there's no better way to learn history. In this more familiar sense, we can define history as our written description of what we have discovered about the past. We have chosen to study specific aspects of the past because they interest us. Whether that interest be ancient China, women's suffrage, the Declaration of Independence, or life in a medieval castle, we must turn to the information left us from the past in order to learn and to understand. Fortunately, since western civilization has been especially interested in recovering the past for some three centuries, we have a great number of available books and articles, in addition to artifacts. Instead of always needing to turn to primary sources themselves, we can turn to the writings of our contemporaries to learn both about the past and about the way current writers have studied and interpreted the past. **When we write about this secondary material, we are entering into the discourse of history by adding our own perspectives.**

But, why should *I* write if I don't plan to become a professional historian?

After all, you enrolled in a history course, not a writing workshop. And now, you look at the course syllabus and find that you're expected to produce a lot of writing — everything from brief biographies and book reviews to the research paper.

Why?

Writing will help you learn history. You've probably discovered the principle behind this fact already: we learn best, not as passive recipients of lectures and textbooks, but as active participants, making meaning for ourselves. And writing is one of the best ways to get involved in your own education. That's what this book is all about — writing to learn.

Your personal involvement through writing will lead you to a fuller understanding of history. Reading, thinking, and writing go together in learning and doing history. Historian Edward Hallett Carr describes history as "a continuous process of interaction between the historian and his facts, an unending dialogue between the present and the past." Writing is the best way for you to enter that dialogue.

Writing clarifies your understanding of the subject. Let's say you read a chapter in your textbook or listen to a fifty-minute lecture on the significance of the Norman Conquest and understand most of it. Writing what you comprehend helps you review, organize, and remember the material. But some of the information still puzzles you. By putting your questions on paper, by writing about your confusion, you begin to see just where the difficulty lies. Often, you can write your way to understanding. Even if that doesn't work, you'll know which sections of the chapter to reread or which notes to review. You can ask your professor an intelligent question: for instance, if the Bayeux Tapestry was woven in France after the Norman Conquest, how reliable is it as a source for the Battle of Hastings? or, what other sources of information do we have about the Battle of Hastings in addition to the Bayeux Tapestry?

Writing reveals your attitude toward a subject. An assignment might be to read two articles about the significance of *The Federalist Papers* to the ratification of the U. S. Constitution. As you study one of the essays, you agree with that writer's position. Then you read another article and are persuaded to that point of view. Sound familiar? Professional historians can be persuasive in their interpretations — that's their line of work. That we readers sometimes have trouble assessing what we read shouldn't surprise us.

What should you do? Listing the pros and cons of a given thesis helps you see the strengths and weaknesses of each side. Writing can help you discover how you feel about each treatment. Then you're on the way to defining your own position about the importance of *The Federalist Papers* on the ratification of the U. S. Constitution.

Writing helps you synthesize large amounts of information. The human mind is a marvel unduplicated by the most advanced computer. Still, most of us don't seem to command the kind of memory we need, especially to sort out and keep track of the places, people, and events that make up any span of human history. Making notes supplements memory and provides access to limitless information. That's why note taking is an essential part of research. Further, you can understand how the information you have collected is related by writing about it. Writing allows you to discover new ways of solving problems, matters we cover in some detail in Chapters 3, 4 and 5.

Writing organizes your thoughts. Of course, you already know that. When you have a lot to accomplish, you make a list of "things to do today." When you prepare a speech or a class presentation, you jot down main ideas, then reorganize them into some sort of meaningful pattern. Combining invisible thoughts with the physical activity of forming words on paper helps you to see what you're thinking. Somehow the need to commit your thinking to the page focuses your thoughts.

Learning through writing leads to fuller understanding of the subject. You'll like this new-found control of your studies. Studying, thinking, and writing history are difficult. It takes thoughtful probing to develop a rich historical perspective. Many people are not able to sustain the effort it takes. You've taken charge when you are able to develop your own historical perspective for use in your daily life — an accomplishment that enriches a lifetime.

YOU AND THE WRITING PROCESS

Has this ever happened to you? Your professor assigns a paper in Nineteenth-Century African history, due at the end of the semester. You're not told much more about it — perhaps you get a list of acceptable topics or learn it's to be around 15 pages long. Then, despite your best intentions, you wait until a couple of days before the due date to get started. An old and sad story.

There are better ways of doing things. Whether you need to write a term paper, a seminar presentation, or a book review — virtually any communication, in fact — the most effective means is the **process approach.** Using this method of composition, you work your way through three broad stages: **prewriting, drafting,** and **revising.** Most experienced writers work this way, even though the stage model or linear representation of writing is not the most accurate way to represent what seems to happen: actually writing from beginning idea to finished essay or book looks a lot more like a drunken circle than like a straight line — in other words, it's full of stops and starts, backward and sideways and forward motions. Very messy! Still, student writers seem to make the greatest improvement when they practice composing in this fashion, knowing that there are many steps to go through before the finished piece of writing emerges.

Prewriting

All the preparations the writer makes before starting to draft — that's what we mean by prewriting. Among these preparations are finding a topic in such ways as free writing in a class journal, limiting that topic to manageable size, defining purpose, assessing audience, choosing a point of view, researching or interviewing, taking notes, and talking about your ideas with friends, classmates, and your teacher. This prewriting stage of the process is much more crucial than many realize. When you recognize that, you're ahead of the rest. And when you master these preparations, you win a new control over your writing. You'll take the first steps in the next section, *The Writer's Decisions,* and in Chapter 2, *Journal Writing in History.* You will also find help with prewriting in chapters 3, 4, and 5, as you learn how to jot down ideas, plans, and outlines and to write a discovery draft.

Drafting

The second stage of the composing process, drafting, is what most people have in mind when they think of writing. Drafting is getting the words down on paper, much easier when you use the process approach. Chapters 3, 4, and 5 will also guide you through this stage. Some people find that they start writing before they're absolutely sure about where the material is going; they need to write to find out, or to discover the focus for drafting.

Revising

Revising, the third stage, involves much more than most student writers suspect. Example: this chapter is now in its sixth draft. In other words, it has been revised five times. That's why professional writers have such big wastebaskets — they keep working on a piece until it's right. If you were to look up the word "revise" in the dictionary, you would find that it comes from the Latin *revidere* — to see again. True revision means just that, seeing again, looking once more at a draft with a willingness to consider changes, often big changes. This chapter has been totally reorganized from what its order was in the first draft, for example. You'll learn more about making these changes as you proceed through this book. Then, after you've revised your way to a good piece of work, refer to Chapter 8, *A Concise Guide to Usage,* and Chapter 9, *Make Punctuation Work for You,* for help with editing. Editing and proofreading are the final steps before submitting your work to reader, teacher, or editor.

THE WRITER'S DECISIONS

During the prewriting phase, before beginning to draft, the writer confronts several questions: Why am I writing this? Who's going to read it? What will they be expecting? How should my voice sound? Consciously or not, writers must answer these questions each time they sit down to write. Whether you are researching a term paper for your European Civilization course, or applying to law school, or writing a textbook for a course in South American history, the questions are the same. Only the answers are different.

What is this piece about?

Your answer to this question establishes the **subject,** the true topic of this piece of writing.

Why am I writing this? What do I want this to do?

In answering these questions you make decisions about purpose. **Purpose** is your intent, the reason that moves you to write and the desired result of that effort.

Who am I writing this for?

The answer to this question identifies your audience. **Audience** is the reader or readers you are addressing.

Who am I as I write this?

The answer to this question describes your voice. **Voice** is the character, personality, and attitudes you project toward your subject, toward your purpose, and toward your audience.

Subject, purpose, audience, and voice are controls in any job of writing. Once you make decisions or accept conditions concerning their natures, you establish certain parameters. Style, tone, readability, even organization and use of examples, are all governed by these initial choices.

The diagram below attempts to show how the four decisions relate to each other. At the heart of the large circle is **subject,** the focus of any piece of writing and usually the writer's first decision. The broken lines suggest the influence that subject has on purpose, audience, and voice, as well as the relationship they have to one another.

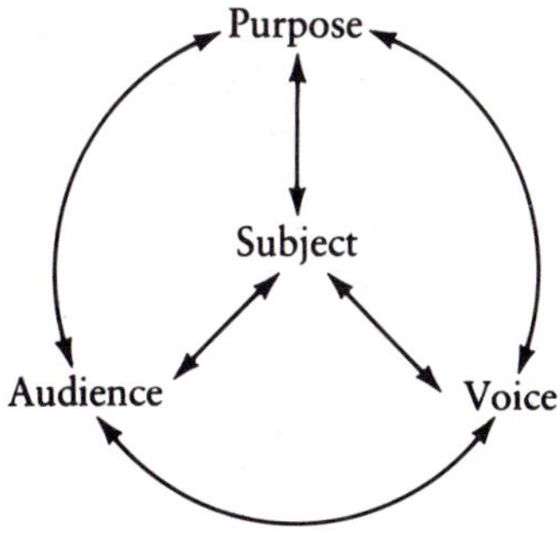

Figure 1.1 *The writer's decisions.*

Decision 1: Subject

Finding something to write about is often the hardest of the prewriting tasks for most writers. In the "real world," of course, you would write only when you had something to say and felt the need to express it to others. In college courses, however, you are often told to write, whether you need to or not. That's because your professors view the writing process as a means of learning. One objective in most history courses is learning to perceive the world as a historian. That means asking the questions and formulating the problems in the same ways that a practicing historian does, another way to learn how to enter the ongoing dialogue of historical discourse. One of the best solutions to this problem of finding a **subject** is to anticipate it. Keeping a history journal will provide you with dozens of ideas for writing as you read, listen, and think. In Chapter 2, *Journal Writing in History,* you'll learn how to make the most out of keeping a history journal and using informal writing to help your formal writing.

Whatever subject you choose to write about should meet the following specifications:

1. It should fit the assignment. Does the subject fall into the scope of the course? A paper on Canada's role in World War II or on church and state relationships in the United States, for instance, is inappropriate for a course about England under Victoria. Does the paper come within the limits established by the assignment? An account of trench warfare in World War I would not fit the assignment, "Write a paper about the effect of nuclear arms on the role of the United Nations in the second part of the twentieth century."

2. It should be of interest to you. An obvious criterion, but one that students often overlook. If you are to spend thirty or forty hours researching and writing a paper, you should feel some intellectual excitement about the subject. Of course you might discover a new interest as you read about a topic you thought dull at first. But to the extent possible, begin with a question you genuinely want to answer. Historian Daniel Boorstin asked such questions as "Why didn't the Chinese 'discover' Europe or America?" to focus on in his recent book, *The Discoverers.* A student recently started asking questions about the Unitarian Church's role in the underground railroad. She eventually ended up with a major senior paper on abolitionism in Vermont.

3. It should be limited to allow adequate depth and breadth of coverage. If the assignment calls for a six to eight page paper, a topic like "the relationship between France and the U. S. since the second half of the eighteenth century" is doomed. Trying to cover two hundred years of relations between two very different countries is hopeless. Limiting that broad topic could yield some very workable subjects, such as "Thomas Jefferson's role in the beginnings of the French Revolution," for example, or "how French financing of revolution in the American colonies weakened the English monarchy."

> WRITING 1.1: FINDING A SUBJECT. Just for practice, you might try to write a list of five topics, suitable for a six to eight page paper, from the following broad subject: The relationship between France and the United States since the late eighteenth century.

Decision 2: Purpose

The **purpose** of a piece of writing can be complex, for it includes both the reason that moves you to write and the desired outcome. If you're writing a book review because your professor told you to, the professor's requirement provides one dimension of purpose. Yet that requirement may not provide sufficient purpose to generate an effective review. You need to question yourself more closely: Why am I asked to write this? What does a book review do as an assignment in a history course that is similar to or different from one that is published in a newspaper or a magazine? You may then decide that you were asked to do the review to get you to read the book, think about it, locate it within the context of the course, and summarize the main points of the book and their relationships to the course.

Very likely all the history writing you will ever do will have as its general purpose either to narrate, to explain, or to persuade. A further classification of kinds of explanation or exposition, as it is often called, will be useful even though writers rarely use only one approach in any single piece of writing. Actually, exposition more often blends techniques to fit the needs and demands of the direction the writing takes to fulfill its purpose. For example, in a paper on the contribution of John Maynard Keynes to twentieth-century economic theory, you might need to devote some space at the outset to defining what the term "employment" means as Keynes used it in his work. But definition would be only one of several expository techniques that you might use as you draft and revise your paper.

- **Definition.** Used to answer the question, "What is it?" of your subject. Example: "What is Keynesianism?"
- **Classification.** Used to answer the question, "What is the pattern?" of your subject. Example: "What are the various explanations of the worldwide depression of the 1930s?
- **Comparison and Contrast.** Used to answer the question, "What is it like or unlike?" of your subject. Example: "What are the similarities and differences between the depression years in the United States and those in Great Britain?"
- **Analysis.** Used to answer the question, "What are the relationships among the parts?" of your subject. Example: "What were the major features of the world's economy that contributed to the Great Depression?"

And, if your purpose combines explanation and persuasion:

- **Argumentation.** Used to answer the question, "Can you prove it?" of your subject. Example: "Uncontrolled inflation set into motion forces of capitalism that led to the Great Depression and to problems in a capitalistic society that continue to baffle contemporary economists in a post-Keynesian era."

WRITING 1.2: DEFINING PURPOSE. For example, begin with the broad subject, the French Revolution and Napoleon. Then ask of that subject the questions listed above: for instance, "what was the specific role of Napoleon in the French Revolution?" Write your responses. Doing this exercise should show how considering these purposes can help you sharpen a subject and focus your writing.

Decision 3: Audience

When you speak, you always speak to someone. That someone is your **audience.** It may be just one person, a group of friends, or your entire class. You know who the listener is and can see and hear reactions; you can tailor your talk to that audience, even modifying it according to the responses you get. When you write, however, your audience is unseen and perhaps even unknown. If it doesn't understand something you write, it cannot ask you to explain yourself. These differences between the speaker-listener relationship and the writer-reader relationship point up the importance of the writer's decisions about audience.

Just as you need to define the purpose of a piece of writing, you also need to define its audience. Let's take an example: the chairman of the history department asks you to write a short essay to be titled, "Why Major in History?" If you agree to do the job, what additional information will you need? Certainly you need to know who is going to read this — what is your audience? The professor tells you that your essay will appear in a brochure to be distributed to students. Ah, but which students? Entering freshmen undecided about a major? High school seniors shopping around for a college? Upperclassmen considering a change of major? Although the **subject** seems to remain the same (reasons to major in history), the requirements of these three audiences are somewhat different. You can write much more persuasively and informatively if you can define your audience precisely.

What exactly does the writer need to know about the audience for a particular piece of writing? Although the answers to that question depend partly on the **purpose** of the writing, here are some useful questions to ask:

What is the gender of the audience? the age?

What is the audience's educational level?

What does the audience already know about the subject?

What are its expectations likely to be? its attitudes?

What other special needs of this audience should you take into account?

Only by raising these questions will you discover which ones you need to concern yourself with as you plan a piece. By asking these questions about the audience of "Why Major in History?" you get a much better idea of how to slant that piece of writing.

What about defining the audience for the writing you do in this course? Because student writers often have a great deal of trouble with that decision, you should know the options.

1. You can write for the professor, the most common way of defining the audience of a student paper. The problem with addressing this audience lies in your defining exactly who your professor is and what his or her expectations are. Often, considering only the professor as audience frustrates the writer who recognizes how much more knowledgeable the professor has to be. A brief talk with the professor about this matter of audience might help you see the value of considering others too. At least you will find out more about your professor, his or her special interests, whether or not your ideas for topics would be suitable or feasible — all these can help you gain a more specific sense of audience as you write.

2. You can write for the entire class, students and professor. If you do, you are likely to be less pompous and more direct than you would be in addressing the professor alone. Why is that? How else might your work differ? Here's what one student says about writing papers for peers to read: ". . . it allows students to share their ideas. The sharing of ideas is important because this exchange allows one to view the topic in a different perspective and gain insight."

3. You can write for yourself, as you might in a journal (see Chapter 2). Practically every writer would benefit from producing more of this conversational, informal prose. Certainly you will be writing for yourself in the earliest draft, even in a formal piece to be handed in after revising for an audience beyond yourself.

4. You can write for a specified audience, such as tourists visiting the restored waterfront in your town, people opposed to designating a business block as a national historic site, or all history majors on campus. Several of the writing assignments in chapters 3, 4, and 5 specify an audience of this type.

5. You can write for scholars in the field, as if you were composing an article for a professional journal. The best way to get a sense of this audience's expectations is to read several articles in history journals and take notes on what you think writers expect of their audience. See Chapter 6, *Principles of Library Research,* for suggestions. Considering history scholars as audience can be particularly appropriate for a seminar or honors paper.

> WRITING 1.3: DEFINING AUDIENCE. Again for hands-on-experience, choose a topic you are currently studying, like the effects of colonialism in Southeast Asia or the effects of the War of 1812 on U. S. and British relationships. Write an explanation of the ways that you might adapt your treatment of that topic for each of the five audiences listed above. Be specific about audience expectations and needs and about adjustments you might make. Again you might put this material into your class journal to remind you of a way of assessing audience for any topic you might have to write about for any history class, as well as for this one.

Decision 4: Voice

"Who am I as I write this review or essay or whatever?" Your **voice** is the character, personality, and attitudes you project toward your subject, toward your purpose, and toward your audience. Your writing voice, like your speaking voice, should be appropriate for the situation in which you find yourself or which you define. Because we have so much experience speaking, we adopt the appropriate voice almost without thinking about it. When we begin to write, however, we need to confront the choices consciously and to weigh a number of complex factors.

Consider this variety of possible attitudes affecting your voice:

Subject: treat it seriously, lightly, humorously, reverently?

Purpose: praise, abuse, explain a process, encourage, persuade, complain?

Audience: peers, professor, other military history buffs?

Occasion: formal, informal, ceremonial?

Clearly, these options are interdependent: that is, a writer probably wouldn't ask a favor in an abusive voice or complain to someone in authority in a humorous one. Your task as a writer is to match the voice to the occasion, the subject, the purpose, and the audience.

Just how do you convey a voice, once you've selected one? **Word choice** is one means. To the sensitive writer most so-called synonyms aren't equal. *Abdicate, resign, quit,* and *walk out* might mean roughly the same, but they aren't identical in meaning or in voice. Some words are simple and straightforward, others seem more formal. In writing about a monarch's abdication in favor of her daughter, we would never say that Queen Wilhelmina walked out so that Beatrix could be crowned as queen of The Netherlands.

Another stylistic element that conveys voice is **sentence structure.** A long, complex sentence might be appropriate for a relatively formal treatment of a serious subject for educated readers, whereas a series of short, declarative sentences could be more apt for informal treatment of the same subject for the same audience.

Voice, audience, purpose, and subject — these are the key prewriting decisions. Making knowledgeable choices about each — that is your job as writer.

WRITING 1.4: DEFINING VOICE. To stretch yourself a bit, try to explain what voice you think would be appropriate for each of your responses in Writing 1.3. Be specific and relate your decision to concerns of subject and purpose.

FURTHER THOUGHTS ON WRITING HISTORY

*Thomas Jefferson as Writer**

Even though John Adams asked Thomas Jefferson to compose the working draft of the Declaration of Independence for the Committee of Five because "you write ten times better than I can," it took Jefferson many drafts with constant feedback from his peers to compose the document as we know it. Consider the arduous tasks that faced the hundreds of writers of important documents through the years since written records began — these writers too had to struggle to get it right so that we as readers could understand the meaning of what they were trying to get across to readers. Our civilization would be diminished without the hard work by centuries of writers writing human history. It will also be diminished for us individually if we don't take doing history as a serious act of writing to learn history even if we have to go through as many drafts as Jefferson did in 1776.

---

*James West Davidson and Mark Hamilton Lytle. *After the Fact: The Art of Historical Detection*. New York: Alfred A. Knopf, Inc., 1982. 62–65.

[2] *Journal Writing in History*

TOBY FULWILER

PREVIEW: *Informal writing* can help you read, think, and write about history. Serious thinkers and doers, from early times to the present, have kept a record of their daily thoughts and acts in what has been called everything from a "daybook" to a "journal." Such records can be invaluable tools in the creative process of any learning experience that involves recording, reading, synthesizing, and writing. This chapter shows you many ways that a journal or historian's notebook can help you learn history.*

This chapter explains how informal writing — specifically the journal — can help you think and write about history. Journals, as you may know, are places to record observations, speculate, raise questions, and figure things out. In the following journal entry, for instance, a sophomore articulates certain historical ideas from a new perspective, and she does so candidly, using her own words.

> 11/15 I must admit I really didn't see the great value of the new order of the universe created during the scientific revolution -- until having read about it in a broader context.

*In this chapter and others, we use samples of student journal entries as they were written, except that we occasionally cut for the sake of economy. We do not, however, edit these journal entries to rid them of features unacceptable in written standard American English. These pieces of writing are by definition "informal," as opposed to the more "formal" style and presentation of the essay.

> In history, one idea leads to another and they gradually build upon each other to finally contribute to a major movement . . . e.g., Newton putting together all the info. to completely disqualify Aristotle's universe.

Journals have been used that way for a long time by serious thinkers, writers, scientists, artists, philosophers, and teachers — people for whom it is important to capture and record their thoughts. St. Augustine and Jean-Jacques Rousseau based their "confessions" on journals. Most of our Founding Fathers kept journals, as did authors such as Ralph Waldo Emerson and Henry David Thoreau, whose natural observations led to great literature. So did the major thinkers of our time: Darwin, Freud, and Einstein. Samuel Pepys, the writer, called his journal a "diary." So did Virginia Woolf and Anais Nin. Edward Weston, the photographer, called his a "daybook." Albert Camus, the philosopher, simply a "notebook." Still others have called them "logs," or "commonplace books." Of course, it doesn't matter what this record of daily thought is called. What matters is that we understand why they are useful and how they work.

If you have never kept a journal before, you might have some questions: What, exactly, is a journal? What does one look like? If I do keep one, what and when should I write in it? Above all, what can it do for me in this class? How can it possibly help me learn more about history? Let's look at some answers.

WHY KEEP A JOURNAL?

The act of writing helps people understand things better. If you are a student of history and you write about historical theories, data, issues, and problems, you will begin to sort out those theories, data, issues, and problems more clearly. *Any* assignment can be made richer by reflecting about it **to yourself** in your journal or notebook: What do I care about? What do I know? What don't I know? What do I want to know? What have I forgotten that I might remember if I wrote about it?

Writing helps you both sort out and retrieve all sorts of information, ideas, and impressions already existing somewhere in your head. Notice what happens when you write letters to friends — how often you begin writing with one thing on your mind and then surprise yourself by writing about all sorts of other things. The same thing often happens when you start to write from outlines: you actually start digressing and going somewhere you never intended. And you like where you have gone and now need to adjust the outline to reflect that. That's one of the remarkable powers of written language; it doesn't just reflect or communicate your thinking, it actually *leads* it! In other words, writing is a powerful mode of thinking.

And sometimes writing tells you flatly that you can't go where you thought you could! "Hmm, at first I thought the Civil War happened because of slavery, but really that's just part of a larger social and economic picture that's fairly complicated to explain." And so, as you try to explain yourself, you see the holes and recognize that you need more information. Learning when you're about to step onto thin ice can be a real survival skill — better to find that out in a private journal entry than in a public examination. Then you have time to do something about it: read more, research more, ask more questions, or whatever. Writing in journals about what you don't know is one of the best ways to start knowing.

Your journal will be a place to think in and a tool to think with: use it to monitor class progress, to write daily plans, to rehearse for class discussion, to practice for examinations, and as a seedbed from which to generate research and term papers. Learn to trust that it will do that. Notebooks can be turned into journals when writers speculate on the meaning of someone else's information and ideas. Personal reflections about history can help you identify with, and perhaps make sense of, the otherwise distant and confusing past. Trial hypotheses about social, biographical, or cultural assertions might find first articulation in this same journal. Continued writing about theoretical ideas can develop those ideas into full-fledged research designs.

WHAT IS A JOURNAL?

I can give you an easy explanation first: journals assigned in class are essentially one part diary and one part course notebook. But a journal is also distinctly different from each. Diaries record the private thoughts and experiences of the writer. Class notebooks record the public thoughts and presentations of the teacher. The journal is somewhere between the two. Like the diary, the journal is written in the first person ("I") about ideas important to the writer, but like the class notebook, the journal focuses on academic subjects the writer needs to learn more about. You could represent the journal this way:

Diary →	Journal ←	Class Notebook
("I")	("I/it")	("it")

Journals may be focused narrowly on the subject matter of a history, literature, or philosophy course, or broadly on the whole range of your academic and personal experience. Each journal entry is a deliberate exercise in expansion: "How far can I take this idea? How accurately can I describe or explain it? How can I make it make sense to me?" The journal encourages you to become conscious, through language, of what is happening around you, both personally and academically.

We know a great deal more history than we can usually recall immediately. Informal writing, free from specific evaluation, encourages us to explore ideas and to think about the richness of the historical past. It helps us to think as we write, stimulating our imagination and generating ideas, promoting personal involvement in the process of writing and learning history. As we write in this less formal way, we find ourselves digressing to follow an idea, to pursue a connection, or to come to a realization which did not exist before we wrote it down.

CHARACTERISTICS OF JOURNALS

What's unique about journals is that they convey thought trapped in time — thought frozen like moths we've seen preserved in amber. They have an organizational pattern quite different from that of more traditional assignments. "Chronology" rather than "theme" provides the unity and sets them apart from other academic compositions. But while single journal entries are locked together in time, the collection as a whole may, in fact, transcend time to reveal more complex, often lucid, patterns of growth, development, and understanding. Unlike formal papers, journals carry with them all the time-bound fragments of thought since discarded, modified, or forgotten. Readers of journals, whether the writer or some eavesdropping teacher, get lots of chaff along with the wheat — and learn to find nourishment there as well. In fact, to historians, journals become histories of their own evolving thought.

Language, too, sets journals apart. Some of the characteristics of good journal writing may run directly counter to traditional notions about appropriate academic writing. (We'll look at some actual samples shortly.) Journals may be full of sentence fragments, digressions, dashes instead of semi-colons, frequent references to oneself ("I"), misspellings, shorthand, doodles, sloppy handwriting, self-doubt, and all sorts of unexplained private references and notations. These features, however, which can be both distracting and enlightening at the same time, occur in journals for different reasons than they occur in more formal writing. Journal writers must feel free to write in their most comfortable, fast, close-at-hand style at all times. As a result, good journal writing is usually more fun to read — more like personal letters — than more carefully-crafted academic prose. The more we trust the value of our own informal voice, in fact, the more we will use it to both generate and communicate ideas.

Consider a journal as a place in which to experiment and play with language at any time, about anything. Journals are one place where writers can have fun if they feel like it. The most important thing is to write often and regularly on a wide variety of topics, to take some risks with form, style, and voice. Notice how writing in the early morning differs from writing late at night. Experience how writing at the same time every day, regardless of inclination or mood, often produces surprising results. Above all else, your journal is a place where you can be honest with yourself (and your teacher), so write in the language that comes easiest to you. Here, for example, is a student of European history thinking out loud on paper, trying to explain something to himself:

> 9/26 What exactly is transubstantiation? If I'm not wrong Luther didn't believe in transubstaniation, but he does believe in consubstantiation, which means that God is actually in the wine and bread.

SUGGESTIONS FOR KEEPING JOURNALS

The following list provides ideas for starting and keeping academic journals in virtually any subject area in college. But remember, these are just suggestions, not commandments. In truth, journals can look like and be anything you or your teacher wish.

1. Buy a comfortable (8½″ × 11″) looseleaf notebook.
2. Divide it into three sections: class entries, readings, and personal questions.
3. Date each entry; include time of day.
4. Write in your most comfortable, informal style.
5. Write regularly, daily if possible.
6. Write long entries, a new full page each time.
7. Collect quotes, clippings, scraps of interest.
8. At the end of the term, add page numbers, titles for each entry, table of contents, and an introduction.

WHAT TO WRITE

Journals are capable of containing any or all modes of symbolic thought which can be written or diagrammed. However, they are especially useful for encouraging the very modes of thought most valued in the academic community. The following suggestions may give you some ideas for things to try out in your journal:

1. Observation. Use the journal to record, in your own language, what you see. The simplest observations are sensory experiences, primarily visual, but also aural, tactile, and the like, and might be most useful when visiting a historical place or museum. A history student will find a journal especially helpful to practice close observation of ideas presented in class texts and films. Note, for example, this entry written in five minutes, in class, immediately following a filmstrip:

> I found the change from Romanesque to Gothic fascinating since it was such a big change. The Romanesque cathedrals were plain and unadorned. They had thick walls w/ very small windows (large windows

> would have weakened the structure of the walls). Since not much light came in they were very gloomy.
>
> On the other hand the Gothic church is totally the opposite. Since the walls are no longer supporting the heavy ceiling, large windows can be put in. The Gothic church has much more detail: lacework, sculptures, rose windows. The doors of the Gothic church are set in to make the visitor feel welcome.

Here, the student both records the particular details she has noticed in the film images and also the concepts which give meaning to the details — an entry perhaps useful in preparing for a future examination or in searching for a paper topic.

The key to good observation is being there, finding words to capture what you witness, and being able to re-experience it when you see it recorded. In most academic subjects, observation is a crucial means of collecting data; journals can help you both collect and think about what you collect. Look for details, examples, measurements, analogies, and descriptive language including color, texture, size, shape, and movement.

2. Speculation. Use your journal to wonder "What if?" Speculation, in fact, is the essence of good journals, perhaps the very reason for their existence and importance. Journals allow writers to speculate freely, without fear of penalty. Bad speculation and good. Silly as well as productive. Because the bad often clears way for the good and the silly sometimes suggests the serious. Use your journal to think hard about whatever possibilities — no penalties here for free thinking or imagining. Look at the first part of a page-long entry written by a student wondering about the execution of Mary Queen of Scots:

> 10/9 Can you imagine the feelings, emotions, and thoughts that were going through Mary's head as she was about to lose it? She must have been happy about her stunts, her blood-red clothing, her wig, but could she have been caught up in her tricks so much as to overshadow her imminent death? . . . was Mary a martyr? Well yes she was, she died because

> of her deep profession of her Catholic faith. Yet it wasn't only her Catholic faith but also her political activities related to her religion.

3. Questions. Express your curiosity in writing; good thinkers ask lots of questions, perhaps more than they are able to answer. Questions indicate that something is happening — in this case, that there may be some disequilibrium or uncertainty in your mind, and that you are willing to explore it through language. Again, the ability to *see* one's questions certainly helps one sharpen, clarify, and understand them better. Sometimes writers use journals to record their doubts and uncertainties — one of the few places in the academic world where such frank admissions of ignorance have a place. (It may be all right to admit orally, after class, that you don't know an answer or understand something; it is something else altogether to admit that on an examination or in a formal essay.) In the journal one expects to write about what one does not know as well as what one does. Another name for a journal? A doubt book. Don't be afraid to write "What's that supposed to mean?" and "I just don't get this." In fact, in journals, it's as important to ask such questions as to answer them. In the following entry we see a student going back and forth between questions and possible answers:

> I don't really understand the difference between a serf and a slave. Supposedly serfs are quite different than slaves, but I don't really think so. Slaves aren't free and serfs are, but still they have to work the land for the vassal and then give most of their produce to the lord. They're given a certain amount of land, but it really isn't theirs. . . . But after the feudal system started to wear off and money came on the scene, lots of serfs were left on the wayside with no work. Because the lord paid them for work and when it was finished he let them go -- I guess that is the main difference between serfs & slaves -- slaves had no freedom or money of their own & couldn't work where they wanted to -- but serfs could.

Other questions of serious concern to the writer may stray from the academic subject, but nevertheless have great value to the writer's social and intellectual development. Journals are wonderful places to catch these questions too:

> 9-16 If there ever was a nuclear war, what life would survive? Would insects repopulate the world? Would there be a new age of De-Evolution?

4. Awareness. Learn who you are, record where you are, think about where you want to go. Be conscious of yourself as a learner, thinker, or writer. Self-awareness is a necessary precondition to both higher-order reasoning and mature social interactions. Journals are places where writers can actually monitor and witness the evolution of this process. You can encourage yourself to become more aware by asking lots of questions and trying out lots of answers: "What am I learning in here? What do I remember about today's lecture? The assigned reading? What has any of this got to do with reality? With me? Why do I want to be a scientist, anyway? Or to get this college degree?"

5. Connections. Use the journal to make the study of any academic subject relevant to everything else in your life — or try to. Can you make connections? Force connections? Find easy connections? To other courses or other events in your life? Journals encourage such connecting because no one is insisting that writers stick to one organized, well-documented subject. Connections can be loose or tight, tangential or direct; the point is, they are connections made by the writer (you), not somebody else. Digressions are also connections; they indicate that something is happening to trigger your memory, to bring forth information and ideas stored in your long-term memory. In journals, value them. In the following entry, a student who has been reading Herbert Butterfield's "math vs. myth" argument discovers his own historical bias in viewing a culture now more than three hundred years in the past:

> 11/12 I am amused to think that the society of the 16th & early 17th cent. actually believed the myths to be truthful. I am also judging their society and inadvertently comparing it to my own. I take for granted many advances made during the scientific revolution -- especially concerning the field of

> mathematics. . . . The mathematical advances didn't only change men's thinking toward science, but also in reference to daily life and mythological belief.

Another kind of connection occurs when you begin to see one subject in terms of another; the study of history *is* related to the study of philosophy, religion, the arts, and so on. The following example shows a student finding this out:

> 11/2 As the semester continues, I keep learning about history and its background from other classes. For example, in Philosophy 3 we are now discussing Nietzsche, his refutation of Descartes & the Platonic-Christian ideals in society and his famous "God is Dead."

6. Dialogue. Talk to your teacher through the journal. Have a conversation, find out some things about each other — things perhaps too tangential or personal for class, but which build relationships all the same. When journals are assigned by instructors in academic settings, there is an explicit contract between student and teacher that entries related to thinking about history will be shared. Consider this journal as "dialogical." Do not expect absolute, complete candor of each other — that's unrealistic anywhere anyhow. But journals can help you learn more about each other as co-learners if you share entries from time to time, either out loud in class or privately through written responses in the journal itself. Here's a student expressing her difficulty with a paper topic, asking for help:

> 12/6 I'm trying to write my paper on changes over the years about historians arguing over Andrew Jackson's treatment of the Indians. It gets so confusing and sometimes I don't even feel I'm understanding what I read. Could I bring all my stuff in and talk to you? I hate to sound so dumb. I can't even get straight all the different definitions of what Jacksonian America is!

7. Information. Collect and comment on everything you can find that relates to history. Ironically, in a journal the straight factual information may seem like the least interesting material you collect; usually it serves more as record than anything else. A former student called the pages in which he recorded lecture notes

"Cliff Notes stuff" and wished it was in his class notebook, not his journal. However, such references — especially when connected with some personal reaction — supply writers with valuable insights about otherwise rather distant material. In a history class, for instance, you might create a special section of your journal and label it "Topics for Further Investigation," where you collect ideas run across in readings or travels; such topics can provide ideas for research and study in the future; the journal is a natural place to keep them. In a journal, unlike a class notebook, however, you want to record information in your own words, therefore increasing your chances of both understanding and remembering the ideas being studied. Here's an example from a student's reading journal:

```
9/5  Europeans were by no means the pioneers of hu-
man civilization -- 1/2 of recorded history passes
before many Europeans could read or write. Until
after 2000 B.C. Europe was in the Neolithic or New
Stone Age -- the age in which human beings learned
to make and use tools, build houses, plant seeds, &
harvest.
```

8. Revision. Consider your journal as a place in which to rethink previous ideas. Try looking back in your journal and see if you can locate where you have since changed your mind on a subject written about earlier. Then write about what you now think and why you changed your mind. Anne Berthoff, a professor at the University of Massachusetts, advocates what she calls a "double-entry journal," in which writers return periodically to reflect upon previous entries. In other words, build opportunities for revision into the journal itself. At other times, consider the journal as a place in which to start formal papers — to make several starts — until one idea begins to develop a life of its own. Then go with that one as far as you can until it bursts loose from your journal altogether. A good place for first drafts to come from. In the following entry, a student is reacting to an idea recorded just two days earlier and modifying it in light of new information:

```
9/17  In my last entry . . . I reflected upon the
Renaissance in Italy and came to the conclusion
that the Italians took the classical works and
started new literary and artistic work with a new
```

> character towards secularism. But then in class yesterday, I started to really wonder how I could be so confused, as you were emphasizing the fact that . . . the philosophies of the Greeks and Romans were being applied newly to Christianity. . . . The Renaissance outside of Italy . . . does seem to me to be much more religiously oriented than I had understood it to be. I think I have it straight now.

9. Problem Posing and Solving. Use your journal to pose as well as solve historical problems. Don't make the posing something only teachers and experts do; use your journal to help here. Whether the problem is posed well, or whether the solution actually works, matters little. (If the problems are consistently ill-defined and the solutions always off base, that does matter, but here the journal will be invaluable in another way, as an early clue to where you are really having trouble.) According to Brazilian educator Paulo Friere, individuals must articulate problems in their own language in order to experience significant growth; journals are, perhaps, the best place in the academic world in which to do that. Evidence of posing and solving problems — whether historical, literary, social, scientific, or mechanical — suggests that you're alive, thoughtful, and committed.

10. Synthesis. One of the best and most practical activities to do with your journal is to synthesize, daily and weekly, what's going on in your study of history: "How does this lecture relate to the last one? What do I expect next time? How does class discussion relate to the stated objectives on the syllabus?" Your written answers to any of these questions can easily generate comments to share with both class and teacher. If you can take even 5 minutes at the end of each discussion or lecture — or stay in your seat 5 minutes after class — you can catch perceptions and connections that will otherwise escape as you run off to another class, lunch, or a quick snooze back at your room. Journals invite you to put together what you learn. In the following entry, we see the kind of synthesis possible when a student connects past to present, ideas to events:

> 10/21 Just as the Puritans wanted religious toleration, so did Cromwell in 1649. Both failed, Crom-

```
well gave the rel. freedom to all except unitari-
ans, atheists, Roman Catholics & Anglicans. To whom
did he give freedom? The Puritans. . . . If they
truly wanted rel. toleration -- why give it to just
the Puritans -- it caused unrest in Scotland & Ire-
land, leading to the dissention b/t the countries
of England and Ireland to this day. It's a paradox.
```

KEEPING A RESEARCH LOG

Many researchers find that keeping a log about the research and writing processes that go into a formal paper, especially an extensive research project, helps them to understand and to accomplish their research and writing tasks more effectively. There's something about thinking on paper in a systematic way about what you're doing that seems to help. Basically, keeping a research log means recording what happens as you select a topic, then develop and modify that topic through researching and writing about it over a period of time — a running record of what you observe yourself doing as you do a research paper. The journal provides a handy and appropriate place to keep track of ideas and materials as you work. What follows is an entry from a student's research log:

```
April 16.  Today I took a list of titles of journal
articles to the periodicals floor to see which ones
would be most useful. It turned out that the pri-
mary sources on quinine use in Africa were in medi-
cal journals, British ones at that. I was mad be-
cause I have never been over to the medical school
much less to use their library. All I could think
of was what if they don't have medical journals
going back to the nineteen hundreds! What to do
then? But blessed relief -- they had LANCET back to
1862! I didn't waste my time and it was interesting
to read about a medical treatment from somebody who
was actually involved in trying it out.
```

And here's another that expresses the problems a graduate student is having with selecting a topic:

```
1/30  Paper topic:
     This probably isn't the best subject to write
an entry on since writing an entry will probably
```

```
turn into 10 minutes of rehashing the frustration
I've had discovering a topic. Since my topic is to
become either a section of or the preliminary work
to my thesis, its content, scope & feasibility
takes on a slightly different light than finding a
25 page seminar paper topic. However, I can almost
certainly say that I would like to focus on Vienna.
. . . . . . . . . . . . . . . . . . .
The other thing that appears interesting -- a cer-
tain parallel between Vienna & London -- as far as
a similar naivetee of the populace and adherence to
tradition. Perhaps something comparative could open
up an exciting topic.
```

STUDYING FOR EXAMS WITH YOUR JOURNAL

Finally, your journal might prove quite useful when it comes to studying for course examinations. You might, for instance, make it a regular habit to respond to every book, article, or chapter you read as you progress through the course. If your responses include observations, speculations, questions, doubts, or summaries, you can be sure you have a solid record of your own thought to supplement your class notes and perhaps hazy memory. Many students find it helpful to compose essay entries on significant topics at the end of a series of lectures and readings; others look through their journals and expand on topics they have treated through the term so they will have thinking and writing practice on some of the important material before they take an examination. Journals can provide practice. In fact, some instructors who assign journals actually plan to let you use them in taking final exams, believing the resulting synthesis to be an integrated learning experience in itself.

Some teachers assign journal topics for both in class and out of class writing. You can see from a sampling how this teacher's list in a history of science course could create a journal useful as both study and practice for essay examinations:

1. What is the history of science?
2. Which was more important to the earliest formulation of science, writing or numbers? Why?
3. What struck you the most about Babylonian astronomy?

4. Why did Cornford believe that science begin with the Pre-Socratics?
5. Why did Socrates dislike the thoughts of the Pre-Socratic philosophers?

FURTHER THOUGHTS ON HISTORY JOURNALS

Student Reactions

Let's conclude this chapter by looking at some student reactions to history journals. A graduate student wrote the following after being asked to keep a journal for the first time in a seminar:

> 1/14 All through college there were courses which one knew would involve keeping a journal. They tended to be theatre courses or English courses or other such ones that blatantly involved creativity. Interestingly, history, which requires a large element of creative and reflective thought to tie together the scattered facts, was one area of academics that never required a journal (or at least the numerous courses I took as a history major never did). And yet, ironically, there is probably no better topic suited for journal writing than history. By reflecting on readings and integrating class discussions, along with tying in one's own subjective perspectives . . . one becomes much more personally involved in the historical process. . . .

An undergraduate who was assigned to write journal entries on particular topics in preparation for writing a formal paper, wrote the following:

> 10/25 I found that the journal entries were helpful because they started you on the writing track, and by doing entries I gained information and a sense of what I wanted to write in the final paper.

If you let journal writing work for you in some of the ways suggested in this chapter, I think you'll gradually learn to be both a better learner and a better writer. Journals aren't magic. But the practice of daily speculative writing will exercise your mind in much the same way that running or swimming exercises your body. The practice writing to oneself can become a useful regular habit: try fifteen minutes each morning with coffee, twenty minutes each evening before homework, or even ten minutes before bed. You will find writing in it easier and easier and, in time, may find it a mentally restful activity — the one time in a busy schedule to put your life in order. And at the end of the term or after you graduate you'll find this marvelous written record of your thoughts, beliefs, problems, solutions, and dreams. The nice thing about the journal is that it represents a powerful process while you keep it and, at the same time, it results in a wonderfully personal product.

One student's end-of-semester evaluation of the history journal experience says it best:

> The journal entries became, I believe, one of the most valuable parts of the course. I was able to work through a lot of ideas in the journal that never would have been conceived otherwise. I think the journal's value was worthwhile. On the one hand, I think it helped me simply to think about the materials I'd read and the nature of the course so that I was more of an active learner than a passive learner. In addition to this, the journal was valuable because it enabled me to formulate some interesting thoughts on smaller aspects of the course that I think would have been lost otherwise. The journal allowed me the opportunity to learn to some significant depth about more subjects than just my paper topic. Lastly, the journal was valuable as a backboard to hit ideas against to see if there might be some yield there. This ultimately proved a very valuable tool for my paper.

---

[3] *Approaches to Writing and Learning History*

PREVIEW: *Writing in history enables us to find out who we are and what we know. We do so through assigned formal writing that asks us either to narrate, to explain, or to persuade; most often our writing tasks call on us to combine these rhetorical strategies. In this way, students learn to construct historical interpretations based on available evidence. This chapter presents ways to go about doing this purposeful writing in a variety of ways for a variety of audiences.*

After a class discussion about how the second battle of the Marne in France marked the beginning of the end of World War I, a student wrote this in his history journal:

> 11/15 Today something really weird happened in class. You were telling us about WWI battles and I thought about how I might not even be here if my great grandfather hadn't gotten shot at the Marne. He wouldn't have met my great grandmother. My grandfather wouldn't be my grandfather -- I would not exist! I never thought about a battle in a war like that before. You're not supposed to like war, but I can't be too sorry even though a lot of people died.

It turned out that Mark Beliveau's great-grandfather had been seriously wounded and evacuated to a nearby field hospital where he was nursed by the woman who later became the student's great-grandmother. His very existence — his story — was entangled with that remote battle fought in a remote war. Writing in his journal helped him to relate the Great War, "the war to end all wars," to his own life experience. He was able to create his own context for studying and understanding World War I.

Later, when it came time to find a topic for his first writing assignment, Mark made use of his journal entry to write about the significance of the Marne on the outcome of World War I. In other words, this student made the material of his history course meaningful in terms of his personal experience and history. The sense of history is bound up with a sense of story — our own and others.

Writing about history enables us to find out who we are and what we know. Writing also helps us to imagine ourselves to be living in other times and other places, thereby extending our temporal boundaries. In Chapter 2, you learned how to make use of informal writing to explore what **you** bring to any study of history. Building structures of meaning in history begins with your own attitudes, knowledge, and reflection on your own historical experience: what you listen to in a lecture, what you remember from a discussion with another member of the class, and what you read in texts and in your classmates' papers.

Most of the formal writing you are assigned in history courses will have as its general purpose either to **narrate,** to **explain,** or to **persuade** — or, various combinations of all three in the **interpreting process.** Understanding these patterns makes you better able to write in varied ways for varied audiences. Chapters 4 and 5 deal with specific writing assignments illustrated by student pieces that show the learning goals of each assignment.

GETTING STARTED

Finding a topic for a paper can be one of the hardest parts about writing academic papers, even if you've been assigned a topic, because usually you have to decide how to treat the subject. For example, you are enrolled in a history of science course and have been assigned to select a major figure from a list of important scientists; you are to develop a paper concentrating on what you consider to be that scientist's major contribution to the progress of science. You can choose the figure who interests you most, but you've got to go about shaping the particular idea and providing evidence to support your assertion. Einstein interests you and you would like to find out more about how his theories of the universe's structure have affected the way we think about ourselves and our place in this universe. But now the real work begins: what to do with what you already know and what you need to find out more about.

In this section, *Getting Started,* you'll learn several ways of getting started through using the journal, making lists and other freewriting techniques, and even graphic ways like mapping and doing a flow chart. We don't intend that you use all these ways all the time, but rather that, by trying them out, you can discover what works best for you.

Journal Writing

Different kinds of informal writing that you might include in a history journal, such as the entry the student made about World War I, certainly can help when it's time to find a topic. Remember what the student wrote in Chapter 2 about how her journal got her "started on the writing track"? She went on to say how she "gained information and a sense of what I wanted to write in the final paper." One of the first things to do in preparation for an essay on Einstein might be to look at journal and class note entries to see if you speculated about this material in any way that might lead you toward a specific angle or assertion to give you some writing direction. In Chapter 5 you can follow how a student historian finds and develops a thesis through a sequence of journal entries.

List Making and Free Writing

In addition to journal writing, several tested and simple exercises can lead writers toward topics that especially interest them. These methods represent activities that many writers find themselves doing naturally — tested by writers over many years.

Making lists of interesting topics is certainly a simple way of generating ideas. Once you have made a list of potential topics, select one that appeals to you. Make a further list of specific ideas and details. After generating a page or two of information in the form of phrases and words (perhaps with arrows to show connections), make additional lists about this topic under headings such as "what I know," "what I need to find out," and "possible sources." Lists breed lists. Information leads to additional information.

Here's what one student listed to get herself into writing a paper on Einstein:

wild head of white hair

ragged sweater

not being a necessarily good math student (fallacy?)

theory of relativity (whatever that really means)

the Thinker of Princeton (think tank — can't remember its name)

German?

reshaped concepts of time/structure of matter

absent-minded genius

A bomb/H bomb
Pacificist
made us rethink nature of being?
molecular structure
gave new meaning to mortality/universe

The most common and even more useful exercise for many writers is the ten-minute free writing advocated by Peter Elbow, among others. You allow the writing itself to lead you toward something in the course material that you would like to explore. The most important thing is to keep writing without stopping, even if you write the name "Einstein" ten times straight until you can go on. Almost always something will happen, perhaps the unexpected if you let it.

The same history of science student wrote the following paragraphs about Einstein during a free writing "sprint" in her journal:

Cosmology/Shape & Nature of Universe

What fascinates me about Einstein more than anything else is that he showed creation of matter and the shaping of time to be more awesome and imaginative than any allegory could show. The force of his imagination reveals the potential for both human and divine. Infinity as a concept that even defies the imagination endows us with a potency that makes it even more imperative that we not destroy this planet through lack of imagination.

Several others referred to Einstein w/reference to the role of religion and the modern scientist. I would like to learn more/discuss ways Einstein the physicist became, by virtue of what he stands for, a stand-in for the potential of divinity in man -- Einstein as god/man, essence of knowledge, holder of the mysteries. Scientist as god. I would like to try to understand more about how Einstein has shaped the way we of late 20th cent think about role of man/nature/universe.

From what you write during the first ten minutes, select an idea or detail that interests you; write about what you've chosen for another ten minutes. Perhaps by now you're beginning to see a pattern in your language: for example, many of the details and ideas the student has scribbled down above concern the effects of Einstein's theories on attitudes toward religion. Like this student, maybe you can put what interests you into a paper you'd have fun researching and writing.

Mapping

Besides the exploration of topics through journal entries, free writing and list making, there are structured ways to think on paper that even help writers develop useful writing plans. People who tend to conceptualize in visual ways often find the graphic nature of clustering or mapping helpful for generating information and shaping structure. In Figure 3.1 a student's map shows her developing thought connections for writing an essay on utilitarian school systems in England of the 1840s and in Dickens's *Hard Times:*

The clustered material might turn into the essay's structure with the larger units paragraphs, the smaller points within those paragraphs. Such graphic thinking chunks material into potentially important relationships.

Another writer might see the same material moving in a linear fashion as a flow chart (Figure 3.2) showing the direction of the essay's development toward the interrelationship of historically documented information about English school systems and Dickens's representation of those schools in *Hard Times.*

Organized Questioning

Asking particular kinds of questions is another way to structure thinking on paper. We will show you sets of questions to ask about specific kinds of writing assignments later in this chapter, but there is one way to ask questions that is especially suitable for writing about human acts: Kenneth Burke's expansion of the journalist's *what, who, when, where,* and *how.* These questions allow writers to examine a topic from five different perspectives. The possibilities for developing series of questions are immense.

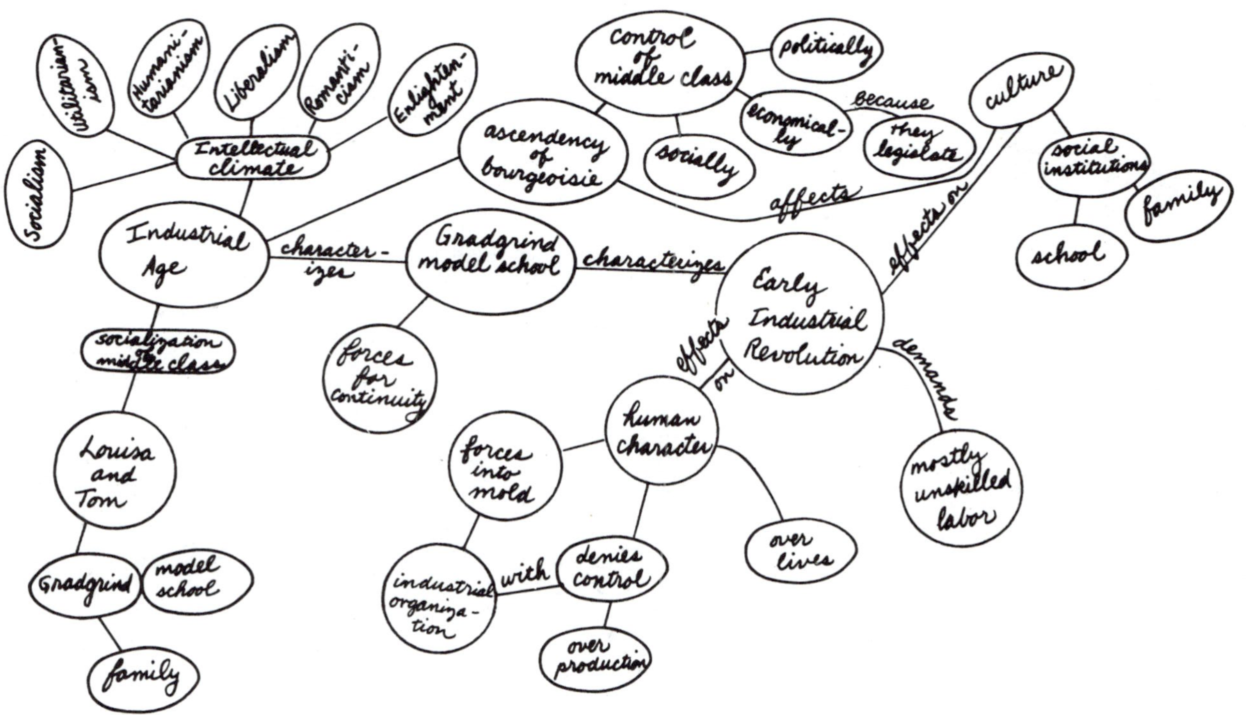

Figure 3.1 *Sample student map.*

Early Industrial Rev. → Industrial Age → Gradgrind model school → Industrial organization → controls people/production → Chartism → Romanticism → socialization of middle class → Liberalism → social legislation → Enlightenment

Figure 3.2 *Sample student flow chart.*

Here is our variation of Burke's "Five Key Terms of Dramatism":

Action
What is the Industrial Revolution?
What is happening? What is it?
What happened? What did not happen?
What will happen? What could happen?

Actor-Agent
What were the causes of the Industrial Revolution?
Who is doing it? Who did it?
What did it or what caused it? or did not?
How did it happen?

Scene
Where did the Industrial Revolution take place?
When did it take place?
What is the background of the Industrial Revolution?
Where is it happening?
Where did it happen?
Where will it happen? Where could it happen?
When did it happen?
What is the background?

Purpose
Why did the Industrial Revolution take place?
What were the conditions that made it possible?
Why or why not?

Burke's questions work especially well for narrating and explaining by analysis. Taking a topic through this list of questions, answering those that seem most appropriate, can even help set up an outline for a writing plan. Topics that concern time benefit especially from being examined from these perspectives.

Writers can also add questions of their own that add more specific information about their topics. Certainly the student concerned with the subject of Einstein will probably add questions such as "What were other current theories about the universe? Which groups of people held to which theory?" Asking questions seems to be essential in writing and learning history. Examples of Burke's Pentad used to generate material are included in many writing exercises in Chapter 4, *Writing Short Essays In and Out of Class.*

Talking about Writing

Talking with others can help us at any point in the writing process. People who write often need to talk out their perceptions, intuitions, ideas, and plans. You may already have the experience of going to a teacher's office with a general idea about a topic and realizing after a little talk that you've got a potential main idea to try out. And how often talking after class and in the dormitory can cause you to hit your forehead and say "I've got it! I want to find out how the Scots went about fighting the Battle of Culloden that caused massive slaughter of the clans." Never underestimate the value of talking about writing ideas and writing in progress.

CREATING HISTORICAL CONTEXTS

The student who discovered the personal relationship between himself and the second battle of the Marne is more fortunate than most of us because it helped him create a context for writing his paper. His connection with the event became his context for studying the war and for finding meaning in this study. Most of us have to do a lot more to create a context — that sharing of enough information to situate our reader with regard to the subject we are treating and our particular attitude and relationship to that subject. A context situates us within our own subject matter so that we know what we are writing from. We need a context for ourselves and for our readers. Likewise, readers need to enter our historical contexts so that they can fully understand what we are writing about.

Context establishes the basis for the relationship between the writer and his or her audience. Establishing a workable relationship can mean the difference between an effective learning experience, both for the writer and for the reader, or a failure to understand the topic by the writer and the reader.

Following are some ways to create contexts in writing history:

1. Consider purpose. Why am I writing this? To whom and to effect what? Examine the teacher's language if she or he gave the assignment in writing: Do the directions include such clues as asking you to assume a particular role and to write from that point of view — a Boston merchant at the time of the Boston Tea Party. Or be yourself and analyze the effects student shantytowns in the U. S. have had on raising campus awareness about apartheid in South Africa.

2. Consider what other history writers do. In her *Life in Medieval France,* Joan Evans establishes the geographic boundaries of medieval France in the opening paragraph. She does this to show its crucial position to exercise considerable influence on the surrounding countries. European geography becomes her device for creating a context for a study of all aspects of French society during the middle ages. Here is how Evans begins the first paragraph of Chapter 1:

> Touching, or almost touching, Spain, Italy, Switzerland, Germany, the Low Countries, and England, France is for ever rich in that force which arises from the contact and clash of nations. Her own strength has always been great enough to transmute and absorb external impulses into her national being; . . . .
>
> *Life in Medieval France,* 3rd ed., New York: Phaidon, 1969, 1.

In his essay in the February 1986 issue of *Scientific American,* "William Herschel and the Making of Modern Astronomy," Michael Hoskins describes "a typical astronomy textbook of the mid-eighteenth century" to show us what Herschel added to astronomy to revolutionize nineteenth-century astronomy textbooks. Hoskins compares astronomy texts to tell us what we need to know to understand his essay. Here are excerpts from his opening paragraph:

> A typical astronomy textbook of the mid-18th century has chapters on such topics as time and celestial coordinates, and . . . . descriptions of the sun, moon and planets . . . . virtually nothing, however, on stellar clusters . . . or the large-scale structure of the universe. In contrast, textbooks published a century later deal with such subjects . . . .
>
> *Scientific American,* 254 (February 1986): 106.

3. Establish a contrast. In the final example of ways to establish contexts for writing in history, student Ann D. opened her essay, "The Renaissance Concern for Order," with a brief description of the medieval mind to show its contrast with the Renaissance mind. Defining the Renaissance mind against the background of the medieval enabled her to come up with a contextual opening paragraph:

> In his statement concerning the medieval vs. the Renaissance vision of reality, William Bouwsma suggests that the Renaissance mind did not concern itself with finding coherence in the universe as a whole; that the patterns it discerned were "limited," "transient," and oblivious to those things it could not explain without inserting man in the center. To imply that the Renaissance mind was not concerned with the cosmic order of things is incorrect. The medieval mind explored its enormous intellectual capacity through structured, logical inquiry; and, giving method greater importance than substance, it asked questions about anything -- politics, economy, personal morality, theology, etc. The Renaissance mind, on the other hand -- at

once assured of immense superiority to other species, and (ironically) skeptical of the infinite power of human reason -- sought to establish harmony and universal balance starting from the inside and working without. Confident of their importance and essentiality in the cosmos -- unlike men of the Middle Ages -- men of the Renaissance strove to give better shape to society as a whole, after it had crumbled into chaos during the Plague. (December 10, 1984)

Again, the writer has situated us in an appropriate and necessary context for reading and learning about a particular historical topic. Also, we have clues about the way the writer is going about proving her thesis.

As the above examples illustrate, creating a context for each piece of writing also helps develop the writer's thesis and particular focus. Situating the reader so he or she can follow the writer's intentions accomplishes another crucial part of getting started toward what the writer wants to say. But it's important to keep in mind that people may go about this in different ways: some writers wrestle with that opening paragraph or so until they've gotten it just right before they can proceed; others have to plunge in and write a draft to see where their material takes them — operating on intuition based on plenty of information. Many writers refer to this process as writing the discovery draft.

WRITING, REVISING, AND EDITING

Whether you are the kind of writer who can only proceed when you've got your beginning well in hand or one who likes to see what happens as you go, eventually the time comes to write out a draft. Some students like to write out a draft in their journals first — or even two or three drafts, each from a different angle, to see what seems to work best. These drafts will almost always be very rough since it doesn't matter at this stage about spelling, sentence structure, or other niceties and necessities. After all, this draft is primarily you writing to you — you carrying on a kind of dialogue with yourself about your topic.

In the following drafts of a student essay on as aspect of Martin Luther's life, compare the ways the opening paragraphs went through changes as Eva-Maria Goy wrote and revised her essay in several handwritten and typed drafts. Here is her first handwritten copy:

October 7, 1985

Luther Paper #1

I think that one of the most important aspects in Luther's life was his being a monk. I believe that if he had not become a monk he would never have been made to think about the church as deeply as he did, and therefore would never have been able to criticize it as severely as he did.

Everything first started for Luther when he uttered the words as he was knocked down by a bolt of lightning: "St. Anne help me! I will become a monk." At this very moment, he committed the rest of his life to a faith which he would later come to repudiate.

Luther's initiation into manhood was so very important, because, if he had conformed to his father's wishes and only gone to a university instead of turning to the church, he would never have realized what, in his point of view, was wrong with the church. Becoming a monk permitted Martin Luther to become very intimate with the church, and very knowledgeable about its ways.

It was Luther as a monk who put the 95 theses on the church door, not Luther the professor. It was the monk who wanted the Church changed to what he thought was the better. Luther the professor would not have thought twice about indulgences, etc. . . . But, again, Luther the monk had to think about these things.

In short, if Luther had not become a monk, he would not have started the Protestant Reformation; he would not have started the ball rolling which would send all of Europe into chaos, and change the history of the whole world.

Note especially that in the first draft (handwritten) the writer talks to herself about what she's trying to do before she does it — characterized by her use of "I" and slang to converse with herself before she switches point-of-view for the rest of the draft. Rather than thinking it's incorrect to write in that way for a formal paper, it's important to allow yourself early drafts to have the opportunity to write through the self-dialogue so that you arrive at a more fully developed essay to hand in. Then you can see places where you definitely need more details and examples to bolster your argument or interpretation.

Student Eva-Marie Goy sees where she needs to flesh out her essay through each of two handwritten and two typed drafts. Most of us need to take pieces of writing through several drafts over a length of time (Goy began October 7 with the first rough draft and handed in a final draft on October 21).

Here are the opening paragraphs of Eva-Marie Goy's final typed copy:

"ST. ANNE HELP ME! I WILL BECOME A MONK."

"St. Anne help me! I will become a monk." As Martin Luther uttered these words, although he did not know it then, he changed the history of the world. At this moment, he committed the rest of his life to a faith which he would later come to repudiate.

Luther was a student at the University of Erfurt, when, on the second of July, in 1505, he was struck down by a bolt of lightning. In his terror, he made a vow to become a monk. Upon his promise came the action. On July 17, 1505, Martin Luther entered the Augustinian cloister at Wittenberg. All this the young Luther did without the consent of his father, Hans Luther. The latter had planned for Martin Luther to live an honorable and profitable life as a reknowned jurist, to marry a prosperous woman, and to support his parents in their old age. But, Martin Luther felt an inner calling which he could not possibly disobey.

As a monk, Luther was very good. One time he wrote of himself:

> I was a good monk, and I kept my order so strictly that I may say that if ever a monk got to Heaven by monkery it was I. All my brothers in the monastery who knew me will bear me out. If I had kept on any longer, I could have killed myself with vigils, prayers, reading, and other work.

But, all of these acts of worship did not give Luther a sense of tranquility, of inner peace. He tried to make up for his sins, but never felt as if he had "balanced the ledger." He did not think that he could satisfy God, hard as he tried.

And here is Goy's final paragraph:

Being a monk and having to deal with the ways of the Church every single day of his life, Luther was able to truly judge the inner workings of the Church. Therefore, he was able to create a credible picture of what was wrong with it, and determine

```
how things should be changed. If Luther had not
been a monk, I do not think that people would have
believed in him as much. Certainly they would not
have chosen to follow him. Without Luther's initia-
tion into monkhood, the Protestant Reformation
would never have started, or at least, if it had,
it would have started at a later time, and taken on
different properties under a different figure.
```

Major parts of Eva-Maria Goy's revision from the first to the final draft concern leaving out the inessential and concentrating on the significant points and providing detailed evidence to support her assertions. For example, rather than merely telling us about Luther's dramatic call to the priesthood, she recreates the scene and its famous words to open her essay. This scene sets the stage for her focus on the priesthood as the real beginning of Luther's life that led him toward events that began the Protestant Reformation. She has become reader-directed as she has polished her prose for an audience, but notice how she speaks in the first person in her concluding paragraph. Here she's not carrying on a dialogue with herself; rather, she is reiterating the major points in her assertion with the assurance of a writer who has provided adequate supporting material. Goy has earned her use of "I."

What helps many of us to get a piece of writing to its final stage is having somebody read and respond to what we've written. As writers of this book, each of us drafts a different chapter, then we exchange and comment on each other's chapters. In a later version, we ask our editor to read and respond. We are constantly generating additional information, better examples, rearranging sentences, moving paragraphs and even entire sections, and rewording. We're rethinking, revising, researching, and editing — all at the same time!

Some teachers will pair up students to work at reading and responding to each other's essays in progress. You can always do so with a friend in the class. One piece of advice: always give a typed draft to a peer to read because he will be able to give better advice with a copy that's easier to read. Also, after a couple of handwritten drafts, most writers benefit from typing a draft triple-spaced to see their work more objectively for revising purposes.

Here are some guidelines that might help you give constructive advice and to receive it in return:

1. List the points in the draft that interested you most.
2. List the points you would like more information about.
3. Write down your suggestions for sharper focusing of the topic and/or for clearer organization.
4. Write down your suggestions for fuller development and/or clearer organization.

From the guidelines listed above, you can see which features of revising need attention first: the large matters of focus, organizing, and developing. These and other questions can help you early on as you revise. Even if there's nobody to act as a reader, writers can always ask themselves the following questions:

1. What am I trying to do in this piece of writing?
2. What is my main point (or thesis)? What is interesting and significant about it?
3. What are the important (telling) details?
4. Have I supplied my reader with enough information or evidence?
5. Should I cut anything?
6. What are the strengths/weaknesses of my essay?
7. How might I go about revising to make the paper stronger?

If you even attempt to write out the answers to these questions and mark appropriate places on your draft, you'll hand in a better piece of writing — more satisfying for you as the writer and more satisfying for your teacher as reader.

In his book *Revising Prose,* Richard Lanham offers what he calls the "paramedic method," simple revision practices at the sentence level. The list also has the virtue of being easy to carry about in one's head. Here's our adaptation of Lanham's Paramedic Method:

1. Circle all the forms of the verb "to be" in your sentences (*am, is, was, were, has been, will be,* etc.). Circle all of the prepositional phrases in the same sentences. For example, look at an earlier version of a sentence from this chapter:

> Later, when it was time to find a topic for his first writing assignment, he was able to make use of his entry in his journal in a paper about the significances of both battles of the Marne on the outcome of World War I.

We revised it to get rid of the "fat," as Lanham calls it, or the unnecessary clutter:

> Later, when he needed a paper topic, he could use his journal entry to write about the Marne's effect on the outcome of World War I.

First, a forty-five word sentence turns into a twenty-six word sentence. Also, we trimmed away a lot of verbiage as we rid the sentence of prepositional phrases and weak verbs. Strings of prepositional phrases, adjectives, adverbs, and nouns often spell trouble when they occur in groups of three or more.

2. Consider who's acting or doing something to what or to whom, or, as Lanham puts it — "who's kicking who." Remember the student working on the Einstein paper for her history of science course? Here's a sentence in an early draft of her essay:

```
Albert Einstein can be considered as the focus for
a broad overview of science in the modern world.
Two of the most important lines of investigation in
20th-century physical science were originated by
Einstein.
```

Here's the same sentence later:

```
Albert Einstein serves as the focus for a broad
overview of modern science. He originated two of
the most important lines of investigation in 20th-
century physical science.
```

Active, more concrete verbs rather than passive, more cumbersome verb phrases make sentences more vigorous and more readable. Too often, much of what we read in scholarly articles and textbooks depends on such circumlocution so that reading means untangling rather than synthesizing knowledge.

3. Get sentences off to a fast start. Instead of "In the event of" try "When." Instead of "I am hopeful," try "I hope." Instead of "At this point in time," try "Now."

4. Make bar graphs of sentence lengths in paragraphs: If your paragraph resembles this,

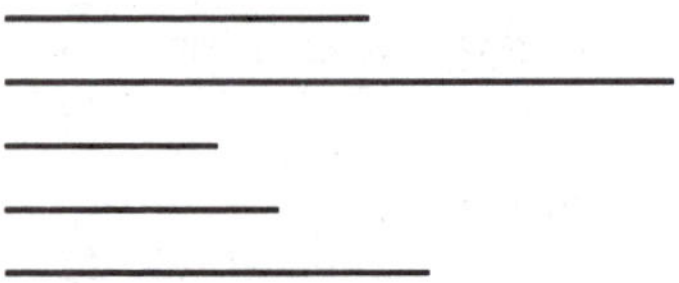

fine. If your paragraph looks more like this,

you should vary the lengths and patterns of your sentences.

In addition to these revision strategies, matters of editing and proofreading depend on your making good use of Chapters 8 and 9, as well as having others read your writing for clutter, confusion, and surface errors of spelling, syntax, and punctuation. Some word-processing programs have spelling checks and other kinds of programs to check your prose for certain readability features. But it's best to remember that you are ultimately responsible for producing a clean manuscript.

USING THE COMPUTER

We've already mentioned how entering your text via word processing onto a personal computer can help you with editing. But the most significant feature of composing and revising on the computer lies in its capacities to make revision much easier. Not only can you revise and edit in minor ways as you write or type a text, but you can also move blocks of material, delete blocks of material, and break up paragraphs — the list is almost endless. A writer friend once said that she thought the National Endowment for the Humanities ought to "endow" all writers with personal computers. Since computer-assisted writing still remains in its infancy, the evidence remains sparse, but its value already shows in strengthening revision practices and changing attitudes toward writing.

If you have access to composing and revising on a computer, by all means try it. Here's how one student describes writing a semester's papers on a personal computer:

> The typing went much quicker because I wasn't afraid of making any mistakes. If an error occurred, I could just hit the backspace key and fix it in a jiffy. . . .
>
> With each assignment, WordStar became easier and easier to use. . . . Two and a half months and about six papers later, I am now able to sit down in front of the computer with no written material and begin to type a first draft strictly out of my head. The freedom to change whatever I want is always at my fingertips, so there is no reason not to brainstorm and get everything I feel to be necessary into the computer right off the bat.

Student Jim Salengo recognizes how much of his planning and generating can take place on the computer screen. His greatest satisfaction, though, derives from the difference the computer makes in his capacity to revise and that, in turn, affects his attitude toward extensive revision.

Here's what he has to say:

> The ease of doing whatever I want on the computer during my writing process is precisely why I chose revision as being the aspect of my writing that has changed most over the course of the semester. Writing on paper limits a person's imagination. All the information is there, but the thought of writing a large amount of material, constantly reading it over to make sure it makes sense, and

> only then being able to type it, not really knowing how many pages it will be, is a very complicated and often frustrating process. . . . my papers are, on the average, longer than ones that I originally did the "old fashioned" way. On a couple of papers I even changed the entire structure by switching information from the middle of the paper to the beginning, all with the touch of a button. It gives one a feeling of power, with a little fun thrown in for good measure.
>
> (December 12, 1985)

Having plenty of revising and correcting power "all with the touch of a button" increases the time you can spend composing and cuts down on the time that physical labor takes. Colleges are making computers more widely available for all their students. If you have access to a computer, by all means take the trouble to master one of the word-processing programs so that you will have the advantages this technology offers writers. By the way, we wrote this book from earliest brainstorming to final manuscript copy on an AT&T 6300 and an Apple 11c in not quite 13 months.

INTERPRETING HISTORY: NARRATING, EXPLAINING, AND PERSUADING

Using the following questions to get started can provide you with a kind of wedge into the subject. Answering these questions can also suggest ways to structure and organize as you generate material in an organizational pattern. In any of these topic areas, you might find yourself presenting material through narration, explanation, or persuasion — occasionally all in a single piece of writing; most often you use at least two of the three approaches as you interpret history in writing.

Writing About Events

An event may be as local in its significance as the day the first train whistled its coming into your town and changed life there forever. Or it may be as worldwide in its significance as the successful detonation of the first atomic bomb in New Mexico on July 16, 1945. Whichever it may be, these questions offer a way to get started writing about events:

What happened?

Who did it?

When did it happen?

What was it like?

What does it mean?

Writing About People

Often writing about a person can tell us a lot about the time he or she lived and about memorable events as well. A case in point might be the American figure John Brown, who has inspired many biographies through the years. Historians have long pondered why a poor white man would sacrifice everything to attempt a war against slavery in the raid on Harper's Ferry, Virginia, in October of 1859. You might examine Brown's life within the context of the coming American Civil War or you might examine the effect that preaching John Brown's funeral had on a Burlington, Vermont, Unitarian Minister and that church's role as a stop on the underground railroad. However you approach your treatment of John Brown, these questions might stimulate the kind of investigation that results in effective biographical interpretation:

When did she or he live?

What is the person's background?

What did the person do?

What are the person's important ideas, acts, and relationships with other figures?

What is the person's contribution to her or his times?

In Chapter 4, *Writing Short Essays In and Out of Class,* we have developed further items to use as interview questions for gathering and generating oral history. These questions might also help you as you read and write about a historic personage.

CREATING CLOSURE

Under *Getting Started* we talked about creating historical contexts as an important feature in beginning an essay and as a way to develop a focusing thesis. Writing effective conclusions is just as important.

Some things to keep in mind:

1. Get started in plenty of time so that as you revise, you allow the necessary mulling time to come up with the most appropriate closure for your essay.
2. If you must write a summary, find a way to sum up your major points so that it doesn't sound as though you are summing up.
3. Examine all the different ways writers compose conclusions. Turn back to Eva-Maria Goy's paper on Martin Luther, "St. Anne Help Me! I Will Become A Monk." [Note what effective titles look like too.] If you place her opening paragraph alongside her closing paragraph, you can see the results of her investigation — you can see the shape of the whole essay through such a comparison. Try it with your own essays. Notice how she even looks beyond the boundaries of her own thesis and anticipates a treatment of a Reformation without a Luther as monk. Be creative with your own closure within the boundaries of what your subject will allow. Consider what each historian you read does with endings — ones that work and ones that fall flat.
4. Notice how we have decided to close this chapter and others. We hope you like reading personal accounts of how historians write history, stories of history in the making.

FURTHER THOUGHTS ON WRITING HISTORY

*Edward Hallett Carr**

In *What Is History?* Edward Hallett Carr reports that friends, both lay and academics in other disciplines, often ask him how he goes about writing history. They seem to assume that it's a tidy affair with two clearly marked stages: first, he spends a lot of time reading and taking notes from his sources; then, he puts his notes away and writes his book "from beginning to end." He goes on to tell us what it's really like: ". . . as soon as I have got going on a few of the capital sources, the itch becomes too strong and I begin to write — not necessarily at the beginning, but somewhere, anywhere." He says that after that first plunge, he writes and reads "simultaneously. The writing is added to, subtracted from, re-shaped, cancelled, as I go on reading." He explains that, for him, "The reading is guided and directed and made fruitful by the writing: the more I write, the more I know what I am looking for, the better I understand the significance and relevance of what I find." He believes, for those writing about history, that reading and writing "go on simultaneously and are, in practice, parts of a single process."

Carr's description of what takes place as he writes and reads, reads and writes reinforces the descriptions of writing processes in this chapter. We've tried to give you practical ways to make your own selections about what works best for you when you go to work to write history.

***What Is History?* New York: Vintage Books, 1961. 32–33.

[4] *Writing Short Essays In and Out of Class*

PREVIEW: *The ongoing interchange between reading and writing history in college takes place through writing a variety of relatively short essays that develop abilities to review, to record, to describe, and to synthesize. This chapter explains some of the relationships between reading and writing that are helpful as you learn how to write a book review and to compose essay examinations. You will also learn how to write reviews of lectures and exhibits, to conduct interviews and to record information for oral history projects.*

- *Reviewing books and articles*
  - *Organization*
- *Reviewing lectures, films, and exhibits*
- *Writing from primary sources*
  - *History through material culture*
  - *Analyzing documents and texts*
  - *History through place: site and structure*
  - *History through people: oral history*
- *Writing essay examinations*
- *Further thoughts on practicing history — Barbara Tuchman on the Historian's Task*

In "Why I Write," George Orwell lists four reasons to account for his becoming a writer. Number three is the "historical impulse." Orwell's "desire to see things as they are, to find out true facts and store them up for the use of posterity" expresses why many of us like to study history and tell it from various angles and perspectives. By doing so, we insert ourselves into the story of the passage of time: the impulse to tell our stories joins that of others to give time meaning.

Among the many ways that historians go about understanding what has happened are analysing books, recording what others have to tell us, and describing what objects and places reveal about the past. These remain important and useful methods to the student of history. In this chapter we will examine assignments about books, people, objects, and places that students need to master to learn history. In addition, we will suggest ways to write under pressure on essay examinations.

Writing short papers is one of the best ways to broaden your historical understanding — that's why most history teachers assign them. Completing short written assignments will be more successful if you consider the following general guidelines on reading and writing:

1. Consider how the assignment fits into the course. Why does your professor ask you to write this assignment at this particular point in the course? What are you meant to learn and to understand?
2. Relate the assignment to the course lectures and readings. They provide the context for your assignment. Review class notes and journal entries related to the assignment; check the textbook and the indices of related course readings to see if they contain pertinent information. After collecting all available information from texts and notes, you will have a clearer picture of what you know and what else you may need to find out to fulfill the assignment.
3. Finally, be sure that you identify all parts of the assignment so that your teacher does not say "This would be an effective essay except you left out the second part of the topic."

REVIEWING BOOKS AND ARTICLES

Professional historians are often called upon to review current books in their fields for journals such as *The Historian* and *The American Historical Review.* They must be able to evaluate the work in terms of comparisons to other similar and related works. Their historical experience of reading, reflecting, and writing about a certain era has been in the making for years. Of course, students cannot write reviews from the same depth of historical experience. But there are ways to go about gathering enough of that historical experience to enable you to write interesting and substantial reviews of books, lectures, and films as part of your study of history.

An important consideration to keep in mind, too, is that, as a historian, you always possess a point of view toward your topic, what we have called "purpose" in Chapter 1. Whether you write a book or an article, you inevitably bring your own background to bear on the subject — to select and structure its treatment to produce what you finally believe to be true about the topic. Historian Peter Gay defines this as "style in history." You have turned your "working hypothesis" (the idea you used as the basis for research) into a hypothesis your written work will persuasively develop and support. In Chapter 3 we discussed the writer's need for a focusing idea or thesis; in Chapter 5 we will show how historians develop and test hypotheses in writing the scholarly article, the kind of longer and more sustained essay advanced history students also write in seminars. It's important here, though, to keep in mind that historians are really always writing persuasive essays. The reviewer must take into account that, however objective the writing style of the article or book, concealed beneath it is a hypothesis the historian believes valid. That's why no two histories written about the same topic ever emerge as the same in point of view, style, or substance. Indeed as Peter Gay also points out: "History . . . is unfinished in the sense that the future always uses its past in new ways."

Reviewing a work of history challenges reading and writing abilities and is one of the assignments many history teachers think indispensable. Good reviewers develop effective reviewing strategies. We can even separate the steps of planning and carrying out review writing into three main categories: **identifying, synthesizing,** and **evaluating.** The "identifying" and "synthesizing" categories draw upon our abilities and experiences as historians and students of history, but "evaluating" may require additional study and research of available material in museums and libraries.

As you are reading and taking notes, the following sequence should help you identify, synthesize, and evaluate the book's or article's contents so that you write an effective review:

1. Begin by identifying the author's point of view. What is his

frame of reference and how does he view his subject? These may be implied rather than plainly stated. (Hint: Often, in a book, the author will describe context and point of view in the introduction; in an article, in the opening two paragraphs.)

2. Identify the author's major hypothesis. (Again, the major idea will probably appear in an introduction or early in an article.) A book-length study may have a complex of interrelated hypotheses creating its focus.

3. What are the most important pieces of evidence (documents, inventions, photographs, first-hand observation, maps, etc.) the author has used to substantiate the hypotheses?

4. Examine the whole structure of the book or article: Have you identified the major hypotheses and the supporting evidence? Are there too many hypotheses for adequate or convincing treatment? Are some hypotheses asserted rather than supported? Is there coherence in the sequence of hypotheses and in their support?

5. Analyze the quality of the evidence offered in support of the author's hypotheses: Are you satisfied that the evidence is used convincingly? Are the sources of information important and extensive?

6. Is the author's point of view toward the topic appropriate? Be sure you are reviewing the work the author wrote, not the one you would have liked him or her to write or the one you would have written.

7. Do you think you will be able to find other works on a similar or related topic? Are there indications the work may be unique?

8. Based on your earlier considerations, evaluate the work in terms of the number and appropriateness of the hypotheses and in terms of the author's use of supporting evidence. Does the author present a convincing argument?

9. If possible, compare the work to other similar works you have read or that you are familiar with. It is unreasonable to expect that you will be able to read two or three additional books in the field or that you have read other works by the same author. You

can, however, think about other courses you have taken and other books you have read. You may be able to draw upon your own historical and personal background to make an evaluation.

10. Do you recommend this book or article to your readers (here, think classmates and teacher)? Why? Why not? Is the work readable and intellectually satisfying? Memorable?

Organization

The actual structure of your written review will vary according to the length you are allowed. Many professional reviews of historical works must not exceed certain lengths, often from 500 to 1500 words or less, because editors and readers want to get the picture quickly, accurately, and concisely. Use the following in order to organize information clearly and efficiently:

- A brief summary of the work, including the author's point of view and major hypotheses
- An assessment of the quality and nature of the evidence the author uses to support the hypotheses
- A comparison, if possible, to similar works
- A presentation of comments, if appropriate, about the author's presentation: readability, useful index, bibliography
- A conclusion or closure which provides a final assessment and recommendation for scholars, students, and/or others who may want or need to read this work

Here is an example of a professional historian's review of a book for *The Historian.** You can see how closely this reviewer follows the guidelines we have set up for you. Also, note how the reviewer cites passages and details from the work he's reviewing in order to support each point of his evalution.

> *The Tools of Empire: Technology and European Imperialism in the Nineteenth Century.* By Daniel R. Headrick. (New York and Oxford: Oxford University Press, 1981. Pp. x, 221. Cloth $14.95, paper $6.95.)

**The Historian,* 45(1):104–105. Reprinted by permission.

Daniel Headrick traces and documents the connections between the rapid development of industrial technology in Europe and the domination and exploitation of Africa and Asia by Europeans in the nineteenth century. He is interested in how technological innovations shaped the course of expansion of European empires, showing how the complex motivations for imperialism interacted with changing technical means to successfully accomplish expansion in different places at different times. Headrick concentrates on three periods of imperialist expansion: the initial penetration and exploration of Asia and Africa by European travelers; the conquest and rule of indigenous people; and the link between the colony and the European economy forged by communication and transportation mechanisms. "In the penetration phase, steamers and the prophylactic use of quinine were the key technologies. The second phase . . . depended heavily on rapid-firing rifles and machine guns. In the phase of consolidation, the links that tied the colonies to Europe and promoted their economic exploitation included steamship lines, the Suez Canal, the submarine telegraph cables, and the colonial railroads" (12).

The development of armed, shallowdraft steamers, gunboats, and their employment in China, the Near East, and Africa marked the first stage of European success. Headrick relates the discovery of the prophylactic use of quinine to the use of gunboats to show how the patterns of European penetration and control of Africa resulted from the combination of these innovations.

The second part of Headrick's book presents the rapid introduction of effective firepower in European colonial armies. He details the production of dependable, accurate, breechloading rifles using brass cartridges, harder, smaller bullets, smokeless powder and steel, and rifled barrels. Such rifles, as well as machine guns and cannon with explosive shells, proved decisive in shaping European expansion in colonial areas. Their use in colonies drastically altered the nature of future European warfare. The "age of raw courage and cold steel had ended, and the era of arms race and industrial slaughter had begun" (101).

The third part of the book, called "The Communications Revolution," clearly demonstrates the colonial impact of steamships, railroads, submarine telegraph lines, and the Suez Canal. The development, implacement, and impact of each of these new technologies is described briefly and interestingly in separate chapters. The final result, in the nineteenth century, was a world permeated by the flood of European technology. In his last chapter, "Legacy of Technological Imperialism," Headrick emphasizes points which were implicit in his earlier chapters. He insists that historians should reconcile their previously separate attempts to deal with the stages of progress of imperialism on the one hand and European technological development on the other. Former accounts of the motivations for imperialistic expansion must be shown to be compatible with the technological capability to accomplish that expansion, and vice versa. Headrick believes that a clearer picture of imperialism after 1880, especially the scramble for Africa, will emerge only after such a reconciliation.

This readable book is its own support for such a claim. Headrick presents little new material, but his emphasis upon the reconciliation of political, economic, and social motives with technological means, gives a broadened view of European imperialism in the nineteenth century.

University of Vermont John Steffens

Here is a student's review of that same book. Notice how the student applies the same guidelines for composing an effective and informative review, yet produces a piece that is individual and informative.

The Tools of Empire: Technology and European Imperialism in the Nineteenth Century. By Daniel R. Headrick. (New York and Oxford: Oxford University Press, 1981. Pp. x, 221. Cloth $14.95, paper $6.95.)

In Tools of Empire, Daniel Headrick outlines the connection between the exploitation of Africa and Asia and the progress of European technology. He observes the low priority to which historians have given this connection. He sets out to prove that the exploitation of Africa and Asia occurred because "Both the motives and the means changed and both caused the event" (11). He accomplishes this task by focusing on items that he believes played a crucial role in making Imperialism possible or cost-effective.

He divides his book into 3 categories, one being the "Tools of Penetration," two being "Guns of Conquest," and three being "The Communications Revolution." In the first section, "Steamboats and Quinine, Tools of Penetration," he focuses on the technological advancements which played a crucial role in the exploration of new territories. For example, he states that in the Orient, the gunboat, which was developed from Indian river steamers and pressed by such men as the novelist Thomas Love Peacock, played a crucial role in opening up that land to Europeans. The triumph of the gunboat, however, was in the opium wars against China. In Africa, Headrick talks of the conquest of malaria using quinine as a prophylaxsis which was indispensable in allowing Europeans to enter tropical Africa.

In Headrick's second section, which deals with European conquest and imposition of formal rule, he discusses items that facilitated the process. In his discussion of India, he shows that advancements in the rifle, namely the substitution of breech-loading for muzzle-loading, had a direct effect on tipping the balance of power in favor of the imperialists. He also discusses the brass cartridge, smokeless powder, and the machine gun, and their respective impact on the imposition of European rule.

In Headrick's third and final section, he discusses the revolutions in communications that facilitated the linking of colony and empire. He discusses how steam revolutionized the transportation links with India, via the substitution of iron for wooden ships, screw propulsion, and the compound steam engine. Also discussed are the Suez Canal and the laying of submarine cables which greatly facilitated joining the colonies with the empire.

It is Headrick's opinion that the Europeans passed on to the colonial people a fascination with machines and innovations which became the "True legacy of Imperialism." This book is a well-documented general study that should force people to reappraise their previous views of Imperialism. The book is written in such a way as to enable readers to assimilate the information easily; after each chapter there are extensive notes which allow for further research in specific areas of your choice.

University of Vermont Brian Cote

WRITING 4.1: WRITING A BOOK REVIEW. Read one of the assigned or recommended books for your history course and write a 500-word review. Use your class journal as you read and analyze the book's contents to make composing the first draft easier. In the final draft, be sure you include the bibliographic information about the book in the same form as the above review, including the punctuation. You may not know the publication prices for the hardcover and the paperback, but this information is readily accessible in the reference area of your library: ask for the current *Books-in-Print* reference.

Optional: If you need more background for writing a review than we have provided, here are some things you can do. Read at least two reviews from two different journals to see how these historians review books. You might also read a review in a source like *The New York Times Book Review* to examine how historians treat a book or groups of books about history when they are writing for a larger, nonspecialized audience. Find a review in which the reviewer describes weaknesses or even failure in a book to see how he or she goes about saying the book has serious limitations. Find out what a review essay is (ask your teacher or a librarian) and compare that review form to the review of a single book.

One student who did this assignment wrote an evaluation of the review guidelines provided above. She thought the "preparation steps were very helpful; also it was excellent the way they corresponded to levels of thinking, building up to the evaluation." The section on reviewing "lets students know what you expect of them, which is important." These general guidelines, preparation steps, and organizational suggestions can do the same for you.

REVIEWING LECTURES, FILMS, AND EXHIBITS

Nowadays, college and university campuses regularly offer many kinds of academic and intellectual enrichment to supplement the professor's classroom lectures and discussions. Posters everywhere! During the semester, most history teachers will take advantage of distinguished visiting lecturers, or special films, plays, and exhibits to supplement course material.

Since these events may be important for the learning experience, teachers may assign a review of a special lecture such as Harrison Salisbury speaking on the long-term effects of the Stalin purges. Your Russian history professor knows that Salisbury's perspective on this significant aspect of twentieth-century Soviet history will enrich the course for his students and assigns a review of the lecture. Another teacher wants students to review a lecture by historian Jacqueline Jones on the history of the black woman in the American workplace so students will enlarge their perspectives of the role of work in shaping the American family.

Reviewing a lecture by a visiting expert always demands preparation. Read some writings the person has done — often teachers may assign some reading as part of the context for a written review of the lecture. Write a journal entry on what you read. What about the piece of writing might offer clues about the historian's presentation? If you know the specific topic of the presentation, make an entry in which you jot down all you know about that topic. Such readiness can alert you to what the speaker's context may be and you will actually take in more of what you hear at the actual lecture. Try it.

At the lecture, use your journal to take notes during the lecture. Try to concentrate on noting the main points which the lecture title will usually point toward. Take note, also, of the speaker's style of addressing an audience: tone and audibility of voice, clarity of points, use of illustrative examples through such media as slides, film, or other graphics.

Finally, in reviewing a lecture, film, play, or exhibit, it helps to talk over the experience with others as soon afterwards as possible to add to your own observations and to clarify information and impressions. Take notes on these exchanges as well, especially whenever there's disagreement. Discussion with others, as well as note-taking, makes the experience richer for writing the review.

Exhibits such as paintings, drawings, and photographs offer history students a valuable experience in narration, since pictorial evidence also tells a story. For example, in your American history course, your assignment is to go to the museum and see the current exhibit, "Subjects in Black Photography 1840-1940" and to write about the lives of Black Americans through the evidence the photographs offer. You must select a particular facet of that evidence to focus on in your review. After looking at the exhibit with your journal in hand for note-taking, you decide that you would like to write about how clothing depicts changing American styles for dress-up occasions like having a picture taken by a professional photographer. You go back to the exhibit to make more specific notations and entries in your journal about details the pictorial evidence reveals that pertain to your focus on changing styles. Later in this chapter we give instructions about approaching a piece of writing from pictorial evidence (see "The Artifact: Interpretive Strategies").

Since listening and viewing are subjective experiences, with varieties of styles and arrangements to alter interpretations, you can express relatively subjective opinions, still based on the evidence you offer. What is important is that you provide adequate descriptive detail to establish both context and evidence for your evaluation. For example, your history class watches American Playhouse's production of "Roanoak." The writing assignment is to review it by answering the question: How does the film present Native Americans?

Again you are dealing with pictorial evidence, but here it is coupled with dramatic action — events in a plot. If you can find out anything about the production ahead of time, do so. For example, where was it filmed? Who are cast as Native Americans? Which Native American tribe did the Elizabethans find in what is now North Carolina? Again, questions help you as writer to find out what you already know and what you need to find out.

Armed with some informative material as background, you will need to be able to jot down particulars about dress, customs, and practices you observe as you watch. Since it may be too dark to take many notes during the film, you will want to write an extensive journal entry as soon as possible. This entry plus background and viewing notes should give you enough material to write a substantial piece on how Native Americans are depicted in "Roanoak."

WRITING FROM PRIMARY SOURCES

On December 13, 1864, Mrs. Mary Mallard wrote the following description of her mother's reactions to the way Kilpatrick's Cavalry was treating them:

> She told them they were taking all she had to support herself and daughter, a friend, and five little children. Scarcely one regarded

> even the sound of her voice; those who did laughed and said they would leave one sack to keep us from starving. But they only left some rice which they did not want, and poured out a quart or so of meal upon the floor. At other times they said they meant to starve us to death.
>
> Robert Manson Myers, ed., *The Children of Pride,* (New Haven: Yale University Press, 1972), 1227.

Mary Mallard's description of how her family was treated by Kilpatrick's Cavalry brings us close to what Georgia women and children were experiencing during the closing days of the American Civil War. This eyewitness report, more than any textbook account, dramatizes the effects of the Union army advancing through the countryside on the South and its defeated people.

Primary sources such as cultural objects, documents, and people yield unique material for the historian to write from and about. Developing one's writing within the context of primary sources such as buildings, statuary, rare books and documents, and people proves invaluable for doing extensive research in advanced history study. But most important, it can be fun, even exciting, to be using one's observation and judgment to gather and generate material in such a firsthand way. These sources make up the riches of cultural, social, and oral history — significant areas of historic interest and ones with large applications to whatever you might find yourself engaged in doing later. We have divided our discussion of writing from primary sources into two areas: history through material culture and history through people and places.

History through Material Culture

Museums on and off campus contain items and objects that yield rich information about ways people in the past have lived. You don't even have to be near such a national repository as the Smithsonian to have the experience of closely examining an object for the history it contains. For example, many midwestern villages have their own small collections of historical material such as early photographs, quilts, town histories, and other documents that record the past. College museums often contain widely diverse works of art: objects such as Chinese vases, Japanese suits of armor, Inuit harpoons and dolls carved of bone, and Americana from furnishings to landscape paintings to Native American clay pipes and headdresses. What we do when we examine these objects is to recreate and understand the context of their origin and use so that we can make intelligent and informed inferences concerning what they reveal to us about the past.

Interpreting the Artifact

Learning history through material culture offers us a hands-on experience with historical evidence that we can interpret for ourselves if we go about it carefully. Again, posing questions gives us a way to interpret through close description and through generated information. Questioning reveals artifacts' hidden history.

One American history teacher had his students visit a local museum that featured 19th-century American artifacts. On this field trip to the Shelburne Museum, he examined objects crafted by people who lived in the first half of the 19th century. He used such questions as the following to generate a detailed description of objects such as a quilt or a weathervane. You may find these questions useful as you go to a museum, select an object, take detailed notes, and draw a sketch of an artifact:

1. How does the object differ from others that resemble it?
2. Does it call to mind other objects you are familiar with? Why? In what ways?
3. What is its size? Color(s)? What material is it made of or from? Texture(s)?
4. From what vantage points can you look at it, examine it?
5. Does the object have parts? How do they work together? How are they put together or assembled? How can you tell?
6. To what category or structure (class or sequence of objects) does the object belong?
7. Was it made by hand or by machine? How can you tell?
8. Who needed, displayed, or used this object? For what purpose?

At this point it may be useful for you to generate more questions about the object you have selected. In addition, museums display objects with brief identifications; members of curator staffs are also valuable sources of more extensive information. Use whatever a museum offers by way of material — even a postcard picturing your object if one is available in the museum shop.

Here is student David Jamieson's descriptive interpretation of a cigar store Indian on display at Vermont's Shelburne Museum:

Jim Crow Dancer

In the Shelburne Museum among the collection of 19th-century cigar store Indians, there is a wooden figure of a black clog dancer. The figure, including the pedestal, stands a striking 6' 2". It is a life-sized representation of the mid-nineteenth century clog dancer T. D. Rice. In 1835 Mr. Rice produced a skit depicting a black clog dancer who had few qualities save for those racial stereotypes popular during that time.

The first incongruity one notices about the dancer is how his black face contrasts with his very white features. The nose of the dancer is long and narrow; his lips, thin and pinker than natural, are parted over a broad smile. His curly black hair (which looks as if it were curled with polish) can be seen below his bowler hat and it also suggests the dancer is a white in blackface.

On the dancer's upper body, he wears a red waist coat with gold bands around the wrists. Under the coat his white shirt is gathered at the neck by a flowing blue and white striped scarf. The dancer's left hand rests on his hip while the right hand is raised above his head; his fingers are outstretched. The lower half of his body is covered by black knickers, meeting white socks at the shins. The bottoms of the knickers are connected by gold buttons. On his feet he wears black clogging shoes, both of which have begun to deteriorate at the toes, showing all five toes on either foot. While both feet are touching the ground, the left foot is one step ahead of the other with only one heel touching the ground.

During the first half of the 19th century, American blacks belonged almost exclusively to the laboring class. Although the innate qualities of being happy-go-lucky watermelon eaters attributed to blacks by the white ruling class were accepted on the plantation, social stratification prevented blacks from participating in anything that might be regarded as a profession. The figure was used to promote Mr. Rice's traveling show and for this reason, it becomes clearer that the dancer is in blackface.

The dancer's name (Jim Crow) was used to identify the U. S. government's policy of discriminating against blacks until as recently as the 1950's. The history surrounding the "Jim Crow Dancer" speaks of a difficult time for black Americans. The dancer also acts as a reminder of the part American blacks have played in influencing culture and national identity. Mr. Rice was one of many whites who traveled throughout the U. S. and Europe stag-

```
ing shows in which they covered their faces with
black makeup. This practice was overwhelmingly rac-
ist, but there were many minstrels, as they were
called, who saw the dancing of blacks as an art and
portrayed them with a comedic dignity.
```

In this essay, David Jamieson focused his interpretive description on the most revealing detail — the Caucasian features coupled with the black face. This detail provides an organizational focal point for the whole essay and allows the writer to make inferences about the social and political implications of the "Jim Crow Dancer."

WRITING 4.2: DESCRIBING AN ARTIFACT. Visit a campus or city museum which houses artifacts relating to your history course. Select an object or artifact that interests you. Use questions to generate information to record in your journal at the museum. Supplement questions with sketches (or photographs if allowed). Examine the artifact from as many angles as you can. Ask questions of museum staff. Record all physical details. Write a journal entry as soon as possible to add material. Is there a striking detail that emerges in the journal entry? Are there any clusters of details from which you might draw inferences? From this material collected in your journal, draft a close description of the artifact. Revise and edit the essay until a reader can both see it and understand the bit of the past the object reveals.

Analyzing Documents and Texts

An American history teacher assigned his students an essay in which they were to go to the library and select a written primary source related to the first half of nineteenth-century American history. Students selected from 19th-century documents such as diaries, letters, journals, autobiographies, memoirs, cookbooks, and speeches. Historian Barbara Tuchman calls these resources "the primary stuff of history."

Again the history teacher provided questions to get students started on generating information. Asking the right questions is part of learning and writing history. The following questions may be useful to ask concerning the interpretation and analysis of a document or primary text:

1. What is the physical condition of the document or text if it is in its original state? Is it an original publication, a reprint, or part of a later collection?
2. What is its publication date? Is the author writing about the present or about a past experience?
3. Does the author have firsthand information? An eyewitness account? How can you tell?
4. Who is the author's intended audience? How can you tell? Was the document delivered orally? To whom? On what occasion?
5. What is the author's relationship to his or her material? Attitude? What clues do you find?
6. Why does the library keep this document or text and make it available? Who would find this document interesting or important today? Why?

At this point, it may be useful for you to ask additional questions of the document or text you have selected. By first asking questions and then finding answers, you may be able to develop workable information that leads you toward a thesis you can develop and substantiate. Again you are attempting to interpret and analyze historical evidence.

Using his journal to answer the above questions and reading such reference aids as encyclopedias and *The Dictionary of American Biography*, student David Jamieson chose a selection from a slave narrative to analyze, from which these parts are excerpted.

In his opening paragraph, David Jamieson clearly links Frederick Douglass's struggle for identity with America's own struggle for an identity:

The Identity of Frederick Douglass

To be born into a free society and
not be born free is to be born into a lie.

> To be told by co-citizens and co-christians that you have no value, no history, have never done anything that is worthy of human respect destroys you because in the beginning you believe it.*

During the early part of the nineteenth century, America was a young nation without a clear identity. There was in practice slavery, an institution that bought and sold men like cattle, stripping them of their identity. At this time, few publishers would accept the writings of American Blacks. The largest bulk of this writing was in the form of slave narratives. "Narrative of the Life of Frederick Douglass, An American Slave" was published at the anti-slavery office in Boston in 1845. An excerpt from this narrative is part of a collection titled Black Voices: An Anthology of Afro American Literature, published as a Mentor paperback in 1968. Frederick Douglass's childhood forced him to create an identity that later welded his commitment to seeing that Black Americans received the same protection under the constitution as their white counterparts.

*"Interview with James Baldwin During the Summer of 1966." Black Voices. New York: New American Library, 1968. 665.

The essay is carefully developed with evidence showing how "Douglass's obscure birth motivated him to create an identity to compensate for lack of parents." David Jamieson quotes passages to support his thesis about the search for identity so that we get a strong sense of Frederick Douglass's growing strength, "obsessed with the need to learn how to read." The body of the essay shows how learning to read and write freed Douglass and aroused in him the desire for recognition of his individuality and potential in a free society. And the closing paragraph pulls these parts together:

> Frederick Douglass spent the rest of his life speaking out against injustices in his beloved America. That the United States has lured people from all over the world has contributed to making this country the admired power it is today. The enslavement of blacks provided a mirror for America to look critically at itself. Once America had decided who it was, America's citizens could then feel secure in their self-view. Frederick Douglass's humanitarian beliefs helped to define America, and acted as an inspiration to a new generation of free blacks. The efforts of Douglass and other abolitionists allowed blacks the opportunity to participate in American society.

Here closure resonates with the achievement of Frederick Douglass along with that of his young country. The historian has effectively controlled his analysis.

> WRITING 4.3: ANALYZING A DOCUMENT. Select one document written during the period of your history course and one related to the artifact you described in Writing 4.2. In your journal use questions to generate as much information and as many details as you can by examining it and reading it; write an entry in which you develop a controlling assertion such as

David Jamieson's about the slave narrative being related to America's struggle for identity. Read your own history readings and any helpful reference materials in the library to fill in material that you may need to supply necessary contexts. After having a friend or classmate read this draft to let you know what works and what doesn't, revise and edit the analysis until you are satisfied that it shows a relationship between the document and its historical period.

History through Place: Site and Structure

As we become more conscious of the effect and influence of environment and place in the quality of daily life, so we are becoming increasingly aware of places and buildings where we can read about our past almost as if they are literary texts. The proliferation of local and state historical societies and individual and collective buildings and communities designated as national historic sites has made us more knowledgeable about the nature of history as a part of our daily lives. As more American students spend time studying and traveling abroad, the greater will be the opportunities for learning "to read" site and structure beyond those which already exist for American history courses.

To put this kind of "reading" into practice, select a building on your college or university campus to investigate. Very few campuses are the result of a single plan and building; most come into being in a piecemeal fashion over a period of time. Or you might select a nearby site that is important for some reason or another — the place where a Civil War or Revolutionary battle was fought, the oldest farm in that area of the state, or the birthplace of a U. S. president, or other notable.

The following guidelines suggest how to go about finding information and writing about a site or a structure:

1. Before you visit the place, write down everything you already know either from a previous visit or from some secondhand source. For example, you are going to visit a nearby park which was also the site of an 1812 battle between the Americans and the British. Since the park is a favorite spot for student picnics, you can write a description in your journal.

2. Visit the site to make your own personal aquaintance with it — or reaquaintance. Before you read any historical markers or guide brochures, find a comfortable observation spot. Look around and record what you see, hear, smell, or touch. Move around and record what you can observe from various vantage points. For example, you are in Battery Park, a city park overlooking Lake Champlain and the site of a strategic War of 1812 battle. Write down what the present park looks like with mothers and fathers pushing swings and strollers, with elderly men leaning over checkers, and with ice cream and hotdog vendors shouting their wares. Write what exists that you think speaks of the Park as historic site — markers, cannon, or statues.

3. Visit the city and university libraries for additional information about the site or structure. Often there may be information in special collections or rare books and documents. For example, in the university library, there are nineteenth-century photographs of Battery Park and a diary kept by a soldier in which he describes life in a tent on the bluff overlooking the lake. What really excites you, though, is his firsthand account of the arrival of a British ship. He describes the firing of the cannon, the number of soldiers and cannon, the heat and noise. This soldier makes you feel as if you are there, witnessing the battle.

4. From your onsite observation and library research, describe the site from the viewpoint of someone who was living during the time. For example, if you are describing Battery Park as site of an 1812 battle, you might select an officer, a university student, a mother of a soldier, or a person living along the waterfront. Here you are trying to enter the mind and time of another — often a type of mental gymnastics necessary to the historian.

5. Using the notes you have taken from all sources and the descriptions, write about what has taken place here and its importance to the locale and to American history. Be sure to document your sources, including the physical observations. For example, the Battery Park site would be treated for its significance to American naval history and its importance to the town and culture of the area.

WRITING 4.4: WRITING ABOUT A BUILDING. Visit your favorite building on campus. With journal in hand, use the suggestions above to find out as much and describe as much as you can. Does the building look the same now as it did originally? Is its use the same? Is there anything noteworthy about its design, its architect, the circumstances related to its construction? Does the college have any materials about the building in its archives? Is there a person whose expertise you might tap through conversation or interview? Are any furnishings original? What do they reveal? Write a paper in which you show a campus building as part of the college's history — from its origins to its present appearance and use. Consider writing it with the college's alumni in mind — even as an article that you might submit for publication in the alumni magazine.

History through People: Oral History

The nearer to our own century we come in our history study, the more likely it will be that the historian can use people as resources. Often people can supply kinds of information that written documents or texts never contain because history is made and lived by ordinary people whose names and faces never get into books or films. In the United States we have some of the kinds of primary sources that historians call "oral history." Among the more important of these collections are the Federal Writers' Projects of the 1930's, of which the Slave Narratives, gathered from 1936 to 1938, are perhaps the most interesting and valuable despite some controversy over their interpretations. In the years since, oral history has recorded women factory workers' lives, farm life during the Great Depression, the experiences of black American soldiers in Viet Nam, workers throughout America, and many others. What these records provide is what textbooks often omit — the individual experience and viewpoint.

Oral history, gathered through careful interviewing techniques and scrupulous attention to detail, is mostly transmitted through writing, though occasionally it remains oral — as do Alan Lomax's recorded interviews of Jelly Roll Morton with Jelly Roll playing his music on the piano as he talks about his early New Orleans days.

The written forms of oral history occur in two ways. The narrative of an individual or individuals is rendered with minimum interference by the interviewer, such as Theodore Rosengarten's *All God's Dangers: The Life of Nate Shaw* and Studs Terkel's *Working*. In both these works, the voice of the individual or individuals dominates and controls the narratives. Very often firsthand accounts become embedded, though carefully quoted or cited, in a larger framework; for example, Irving Howe's *World Of Our Fathers: The Journey of the East European Jews to America and the Life They Found and Made*. Throughout the documentation of Howe's study, there are constant references to "Conversation with . . ." and "Interview with. . . ." Since Nate Shaw could tell us so vividly what life was like in the South for a black tenant farmer and Terkel's working people could tell us what it's like to work in jobs that are often full of drudgery without much of a paycheck, these writers let people tell their own stories in the rhythms of the vernacular. As Rosengarten says about Nate Shaw: "Nate Shaw belongs to the tradition of farmer-storytellers." Many of the people in these books and others tell us about the lives of those who are not accustomed to writing things down. People like Nate Shaw in Alabama and elderly East European American Jews in cities like New York are what Rosengarten calls "a national resource."

If the historian in you can't resist seeking out one of these resources, here are some interview guidelines that can help you gather the most accurate and useful material:

1. Make an appointment well in advance — at least a week beforehand. Whether by phone or letter, carefully explain who you are and what your project is. For example, in your Women in U. S. History class, you are doing research on women in the Armed Forces during World War II. Your retired third grade teacher was an officer in the WACS. You know she's full of valuable information about her experiences and those of other women. If you explain clearly what you want to ask her about, she'll probably be more likely to have pertinent information on tap for the appointed session. If you wish to tape as well to take notes of the session, now would be the time to make that request. To settle such matters in advance is both courteous and professional.

2. Prepare a starter list of about 5 to 6 questions so that you will be sure to get some necessary information and get your interview going in a fruitful vein. Most people like to tell about themselves and their lives, and will talk freely if given the chance. Say as little as possible yourself except to ask for more details or to clarify some important detail. If your interviewee should happen to request that something remain off the record, be sure to oblige.

Here are some sample starter questions based on The Great Depression:

- Do you remember the Stock Market Crash of 1929? the bank holidays of the 1930's?
- What did the people you knew think of Herbert Hoover? of Franklin Delano Roosevelt?
- What did members of your family do to earn a living? Did you know anybody who worked for the CCC or the WPA?
- Does the fact that you lived through the Depression affect your attitudes and ideas today?

Notice how specific these questions are; the interviewer is well prepared.

3. During the interview, note whether you are having difficulty recording the information as accurately as you would like. If necessary, ask if you can schedule another appointment. Offer to let the interviewee read over your preliminary draft. He or she may think of additional information to fill gaps in what you have written.

In addition to their use in writing about real persons, some of these techniques can be valuable in writing about historical personages. For example, you are asked to write an essay in which you select some facet of Martin Luther's life and show how that event or relationship affected what Luther accomplished as the major Reformation figure — student Maria Goy chose Luther's decision to become a monk (see Chapter 3). You might select Luther's views about family life and show how those views contributed to his ideas about the Reformation. Pose a series of questions as if you were interviewing Luther yourself. Restrict yourself to questions that you have found some basis for in the material you have read, either in a biography or in a textbook. Of course, this kind of biographical essay is not necessarily writing from primary sources.

WRITING 4.5: WRITING ABOUT A PERSON AS ORAL HISTORY. Interview an older person about a historical event that happened during his or her lifetime. Find out which event the interviewee wants to talk about and do some research about that event in your readings and in the library. Develop a list of at least five starter questions in your journal.

The written interview should contain the following:

1. Introduction — write at least one paragraph in which you present the issue and identify the interviewee and describe that person and her or his relationship to your research.
2. You may write the body of the interview in question-and-answer format (with the answers edited for clarity and ease of reading) or you may want to paraphrase some of the material, letting the speaker's actual voice appear where it will add the most authority and interest.
3. Conclusion — write a paragraph or two in which you treat your impression of that person and the importance of his or her information to your research and its implications.

Revise and edit the essay carefully so your readers will clearly understand your issue and your treatment of it through generating your own primary source material to substantiate your thesis. When you document a person, all you need to say in the End Notes is: Interview with Mrs. ___________, October 16, 1986.

WRITING ESSAY EXAMINATIONS

Writing successful essays under the pressure of time during an examination comes from careful preparation throughout the entire semester and especially during the week before the exam. Everybody knows that cramming the night before is not the smartest way to approach an essay exam. History essay exams ask you to display both what you know and what you understand about the course you are taking. As a good student, you will want to show your best thinking and most effective writing.

Aspiring to do well and working hard do not always mean superior results within the constraints of time. From the opening lecture and the first reading assignment, you need a plan for writing exam essays. The best way to be ready for an exam is to be an active reader and listener from the beginning of each semester.

1. Practice forming essay questions about the lecture material on a regular basis. Write them down with trial answers in your journal. Thinking about the material in order to frame questions helps you learn the material because it gives structure and purpose, helping you understand connections and implications. Facts, especially dates, need to be placed within a framework of explanations to make them meaningful and memorable.

2. Summarizing important chapters or sections in your reading in your own words helps you understand the material and provides a ready source of information that you have written yourself and is therefore meaningful to you. Think of good exam questions that emerge from the reading assignments. Ask yourself how the reading relates to the lecture. Nothing strengthens an examination essay more than a comparison of readings and lectures on the essay topic.

3. The mechanics of writing an essay exam bear brief mention: DO NOT START WRITING IMMEDIATELY! Read the question carefully and break it down into its parts. Be sure to address each part. Jot down a brief outline or list of the main points you want to cover, beginning with the most important so that if you run out of time, you will have presented the most important material.

WRITING 4.6: WRITING AN EXAM ESSAY. Write down what you consider one of the most significant questions raised in the history reading assignments this week. Allowing 30 minutes and following the advice given above, compose an essay in which you give what you consider a thoughtful answer with examples and conclusion. How well did you answer the question? If you do one of these in your journal each week, you will be better prepared for your next hour exam. Chapter 2 contains some good advice about using your class journal to study for and to practice for exams.

FURTHER THOUGHTS ON PRACTICING HISTORY

*Barbara Tuchman on the Historian's Task**

Barbara Tuchman has always expressed an exceptional degree of awareness about the historian's obligation: in her collected essays, *Practicing History,* she writes that "Events happen; but to become history they must be communicated and understood." In this chapter we have concerned ourselves with that need to communicate and understand. Other words by Barbara Tuchman express what we have aimed to show: "In the long run the best writer is the best historian." The best writer of history will, as Tuchman puts it, exercise judgment in the selection of facts, "his art in their arrangement. His method is narrative. His subject is the story of man's past. His function is to make it known." Learning to exercise judgment about what we read and hear and see and learning to synthesize from the evidence primary sources offer helps us "make" history "known" too.

**Practicing History.* New York: Alfred A. Knopf, Inc., 1981. 64, 39, 32.

[5] *The Research Paper as the Model for Short Scholarly Writing*

PREVIEW: *Writing history with evidence researched from both primary and secondary sources strengthens the interrelated acts of reading and writing. It's also the most intense and valuable way to teach yourself the insides of history — a process of searching, reading, selecting, classifying, organizing, synthesizing, and documenting material to show how an idea works to help us understand something in the past. Writing from research shows that history is far more than a collection of facts. This chapter focuses on defining historical sources and showing how they can help you produce a piece of scholarly writing.*

What is research?

Basically, research is what we do when we go about finding answers to what we don't know — a deliberate quest for knowledge. Filling in knowledge about the human past is one of our most important means of imposing form on the fragmentary remains of human existence — a history made of other histories.

THE NATURE OF HISTORICAL SOURCES

Historical research broadens our experience in a way which enables us to write history with a degree of conviction and authority. And here's where the real excitement lies. One student found newspaper articles from the 1850's that showed how actively involved the Unitarian ministry in New England was with the abolitionist movement. She found that a Unitarian minister preached the notorious John Brown's funeral even though his parish members disapproved. Her findings led her to further research and a paper on the difficulties these ministers faced within their own congregations and communities over their work with the underground railroad — a topic that had never been explored before to the extent that she was able to do. Another student found correspondence between two sisters in the early nineteenth century that related the harsh conditions facing women as they went westward with their husbands and children. Again, an interesting paper resulted that adds to our knowledge of family life on the American frontier and how women learned to cope with adverse circumstances.

Research itself can take many forms. The most common historical research involves reading documents in both published and manuscript forms. As we showed in Chapter 4, historical research can also involve interviewing people with firsthand experience related to your interests — an oral history that can combine with written forms in your research to provide an extra dimension of authority. Theodore White combined these kinds of research to compile his important *Making of the President* volumes. We also described in Chapter 4's section, *Writing from Primary Sources,* how research can extend to the examination of sites, structures, and artifacts — actual physical evidence from the period that interests you. Increasingly, too, the nineteenth and twentieth centuries yield many kinds of visual and oral evidences that add to the store of historical research materials. Artifacts, photographs, film, and other graphic and plastic art are frequently available to historians in the form of showings and exhibits. These exhibits help the historian to understand the context and meaning of the actual physical remains of another time and place, whether recent or remote. Written sources, oral and visual sources, as well as displays of artifacts, enrich the material available to the historian; whenever all these sources are available, thorough research requires their use — primary as well as secondary.

Primary and Secondary Sources

The distinction between primary and secondary sources for historical research is crucial. Primary source material is that directly related to the topic and period under consideration. For example, the figure "Jim Crow Dancer" that student David Jamieson wrote about in Chapter 4 is a primary source because it was made in 1835 as an advertisement for clog dancer T. D. Rice, an attraction in a traveling minstrel show. In contrast, secondary sources are another's description or explanation of the topic or event, made at a later time, usually from a different place. For us who read David Jamieson's description and interpretation of the "Jim Crow Dancer," his essay is a secondary source because we are seeing through another's eyes. David, however, is seeing and interpreting the carved figure through his own eyes.

Secondary sources are removed from the historical event in time and place just as we are removed from the historical event by time and place. Those writers of materials we would consider secondary sources for our own historical research are in much the same position as we are, in trying to find out about the historical past. They, as we, must try to get past the secondhand accounts of the event to reach the available primary source materials. For example, historian Herbert G. Gutman wrote his important study *The Black Family in Slavery and Freedom 1750–1925* as a result of being "stimulated by the bitter public and academic controversy surrounding Daniel P. Moynihan's *The Negro Family in America: The Case for National Action*." Here is a case of one historian reading secondary sources, Moynihan's book and influential historical studies by E. Franklin Frazier and Stanley M. Elkins, and, in the controversy, setting out to examine the primary sources — all kinds of documentary material relating to black family structures and behavior — in order to see for himself. He found sources such as the voluminous Freedman's Bureau records to detail "the powerful expression of affective Afro-American familial kin beliefs and behavior in the wartime and immediate postwar years" rather than to sustain the conventional opinion that slavery destroyed and jeopardized the Afro-American family and that enslavement remains the cause of present troubles. [Herbert G. Gutman, *The Black Family in Slavery and Freedom, 1750–1925* (New York: Random House, 1976), xx.] Historians constantly examine and reexamine primary sources to modify and to justify historical interpretations. Like Gutman, our reliance on primary sources — materials directly related to the period and topic that interest us — allows us to form our own conclusions about the past. Primary source material is the raw material from which we can construct our own account of what happened in the historical past.

Secondary sources tell us about the historical event that we're interested in, but they also contain the writers' point of view, their historical hypotheses related to the event, and their selection of the facts from the primary materials at their disposal. When we write history, we are writing secondary sources for others to read. One way we can produce a primary source is by writing directly from and about our own life experiences, as Frederick Douglass did in his three autobiographies, one of which — *Narrative of the Life of Frederick Douglass* — David Jamieson wrote about in his essay "The Identity of Frederick Douglass." But the history we write as secondary material can also become a primary source for someone after us if they want to use us as an example of how history was written in the 1980's. Most importantly, in order to be a source, either primary or secondary, we need to write some history from sound evidence.

Objectivity and Subjectivity

What is a fact?

Having the primary source material available does not automatically insure that we will be able to write about history as it actually occurred. The term "objectivity" implies that there is some rigorous method which we can use to turn the "facts" gathered from primary source material into a historical account of what happened in the past. The usual model for objectivity is the scientific method.

Since the late nineteenth century, many have assumed that the sciences could proceed objectively from the collection of "hard facts" about the physical world to true and unambiguous general statements about nature. The scientist becomes then a "truth sayer," in command of a method through which the "hard facts" collected in the experiment could be turned into true statements about the world.

Yet the history of science itself demonstrates the problem inherent in this view. The "facts" about the natural world do not change if they are gathered carefully. But the scientists' "true and unambiguous statements about nature" have changed radically over the years. For example, humans have observed and recorded the stars, planets, and comets for centuries. Yet the scientist's interpretations of the carefully gathered facts have yielded at least three different universes: the Ptolemaic, the Copernican, and the Newtonian. The facts remain the same, the interpretations of these facts vary. Therefore, since "objectivity" does not totally describe what happens when scientists do science, we should not expect that "objectivity" totally describes what occurs when we attempt to write history. Objectivity is only part of the process of interpreting facts; subjectivity — all we as humans with individual selves bring to whatever we read or write — also helps us describe what occurs when we do history.

As a necessary and positive part of writing history, subjectivity insures that the history we write can interest us and our contemporaries. Indeed, we turn to the historical past with interests generated in our present. We become interested in either the women's suffrage movement or the Napoleonic Wars for reasons which belong to us now, at this moment in our lives. We possess our own points of view towards topics of interest; we form our own hypotheses about what happened in the past, and we support these hypotheses not with "the facts," but with facts we have selected to support our points of view and our hypotheses about what happened in the past.

We go to primary sources to discover facts, little nuggets of information, and we turn these facts into evidence, not by changing them in any way, but by using them to support the hypotheses we suggest about the past, formulated from our own points of view. Just as scientists have used the unchanging facts about the natural world to produce different interpretations about the universe, historians collect facts about the historical past and use them as their evidence to support their own changing interpretations of what has taken place. Of course, historians must take care to be unbiased in collecting their facts, to use all available sources, and to gather all the information. But we must also acknowledge that the process of writing history introduces subjective factors which give history its interest and character. As we will soon see, focusing our interests, selecting and developing a topic, organizing our material, and composing a draft all involve "subjective" factors after the "objective" collection of the facts. Barbara Tuchman reconciles the two this way: "The historian's task is . . . to tell what happened within the discipline of the facts." But she follows this assertion about objectivity with "What his imagination is to the poet, facts are to the historian. His exercise of judgment comes in their selection, his art in their arrangement."

Rather than the dry-as-dust chronicler of facts, the historian is much closer to the novelist even though there have been times in the late nineteenth century and the 1950's when some historians argued that history could be objectively interpreted. Most historians think differently now.

Listen to historian Nancy Partner addressing other historians on these same issues in writing history:

> All historians know that history is no longer the discipline busily fulfilling its positivistic promise to tell it all as it really happened. And, in fact, that cultural moment, of naive assertions about splicing together an entire, indubitable, objectively once-existing Past, was a very brief digression in history's longer, more richly compromised life as the expressive artifact of tradition, culture, human defiance of time — the whole cultural baggage carried variously and jointly by religion, literature, art, and history. Somewhere in that baggage are truth, objectivity, and dispassionate reason, but as part of the culture, not outside in some preverbal higher reality.
>
> ["Making Up Lost Time: Writing on the Writing of History," *Speculum* 61/1 (1986), 117.]

It's important to know what we're engaged in when we write history from our point of view as participants in a culture. Nowadays we know we cannot "tell it all as it really happened," because our evidence never contains all that existed. We have to recognize this dimension of "pastness" or loss when we attempt to recreate or reconstruct the past — "making up lost time."

WRITING 5.1: WRITING FROM FACTS. Take the following list of facts and construct one paragraph about what happened.

five men
business suits
rubber surgical gloves
walkie-talkie
forty rolls of unexposed film
two cameras
lock picks
two pen-size tear gas guns
several bugging devices
a break-in
an arrest
Democratic National Committee headquarters, Watergate
Washington, D. C.
2: 30 a.m. Saturday, June 17, 1972

Compare your paragraph with another student's in your class. How are they alike? How do they differ? Why do they differ?

SELECTING AND DEVELOPING A TOPIC

Carl Becker once advised that the historian "write a good book about something that interests him." This maxim seems fairly simple and straightforward, but like all proverbial wisdom, its very simplicity belies its significance. Selecting an interesting and important topic is neither easy nor always straightforward.

It interests us as historians to follow Roger Shattuck's description of finding the topic and the title of his intellectual history of Paris at the turn of the century, *The Banquet Years: The Origins of the Avant-Garde in France 1885 to World War I,* in these words from the 1967 Preface:

> This book was conceived one chilling March night eighteen years ago in Piana, Corsica. A year's work on Apollinaire translations had led me to a remarkable poet, and through him to an irresistibly attractive era. . . . Then came the idea — a kind of gambler's hunch — that the trio Rousseau-Satie-Apollinaire represented several significant aspects of the period and could reveal them better than any single figure. The idea would not die.

Shattuck goes on to describe how including writer Alfred Jarry "helped clarify my underlying subject: how the fluid state known as bohemia, a cultural underground smacking of failure and fraud, crystallized for a few decades into a self-conscious avant-garde that carried the arts into a period of astonishingly varied renewal and accomplishment." Shattuck said the "original conception" gave him both "the comparative method of the book and its multiple subject. The title emerged unsummoned out of the reading at an early stage; I never looked for another."

It's interesting to observe that Shattuck's language reveals the origins and development of *The Banquet Years* to be akin to the creativity of human birth. Both processes are complex and exciting. As readers we benefit because Shattuck drew upon his own interests and his incomplete knowledge to think about and formulate a topic. During the incubation period of translating Apollinaire, to continue the birth metaphor, Shattuck kept building on his interest, getting more and more involved in the cultural life of Paris, beginning to consider what would follow the translation period. The topic emerged to take on its own life and development.

As soon as research started, Shattuck's findings began to interact with ideas about the topic. Things he had not known before, such as the importance of playwright Jarry's works, modified the topic; the title came out of the reading. The unexpected always happens as information and knowledge grow.

Just as there is continuous interaction between the development of a topic and the research process, this same interactive process continues when you begin writing. And just as the interaction between topic development and research is constructive, improving the topic and therefore the final product, so too is the interaction between research and writing positive. Here is how one student has described that interaction in the research log (see Chapters 2 and 6 for keeping a log of the research/writing process) she kept while she wrote a seminar paper:

> March 28. Since I began to write before I had finished my research, I am constantly interacting with research material as I write. I have begun my writing early because I have had the problem in the past of never having done enough research before the paper is due (there is always another source to consult). An unforeseen advantage to researching while writing is that I am able to see important information instantly as I read, and find it easier to spot superfluous material. As a result I save time and paper while taking notes. I am also able to revise my paper with material that is fresh in my mind. While I did not intend to research and write at the same time, since I began to do so two years ago I have found it to be a much better way of writing for more reasons than my original intention of beating procrastination.

WRITING 5.2: WRITING ABOUT THE RESEARCH/WRITING PROCESS. In your class journal or notebook, write a paragraph in which you describe a research/writing experience you have had. What do you learn from what you've described? What do you do that seems to help most? the least?

Following Your Interests

Natalie Zemon Davis opens the preface of her book *The Return of Martin Guerre,* a famous story of a sixteenth-century French impostor, by saying it "grew out of a historian's adventure with a different way of telling about the past." Through her collaboration on the film *Le Retour de Martin Guerre,* Davis found that her desire to learn more "prompted" her "to dig deeper into the case, to make historical sense of it." She goes on to tell how the power of film led her toward researching and writing the book: "I felt I had my own historical laboratory, generating not proofs, but historical possibilities." But as the film stimulated ways of seeing that energized the historian's creativity, it also pointed toward other dimensions of knowing that film could not as readily explore:

> Our film was an exciting suspense story that kept the audience as unsure of the outcome as the original villagers and judges had been. But where was there room to reflect upon the significance of identity in the sixteenth century?

Unlike Shattuck or Davis, you sometimes may have your research paper topics assigned or you may have a limited range of choices for a topic. Occasionally you have the freedom to choose any area of interest within the boundaries of the course. But no matter what the strictures of the assignment may be, you must relate the project to your own academic experience and interests. Remember the student who connected his ancestry to the Battle of the Marne in World War I and searched for a topic related to that battle? Here is what a student wrote in her journal that helped her find a paper topic in a course on European Civilization since 1815:

> #19 March 4, 1986. The Relationship of Technology and Imperialism
>
> Headrick's introduction in The Tools of Empire pointed out to me the importance of the technological factor to imperialism. I found it interesting how he stressed that technology had really been a factor which historians generally did not pay that much attention to. I agree with him at this point in my study of history because anything which I have so far learned concerning European imperialism has been mainly attributed to political and economic factors. But what Headrick stresses in his introduction makes complete sense, "A complex process like imperialism results from both appropriate motives and adequate means." Another point which he

> made I also agree with, that within the European colonies it has been technology which has triumphed and not ideology. I find it extremely plausible that "Western technology has transformed the world more that any leader, religion, revolution, or war." I find this to be interesting and I look forward to reading his book and understanding his arguments for a relationship which does exist between technology and European imperialism.

From the very beginning, you should define a context within which the paper will be written. In the journal entry above, student Patricia Tursi is in the process of identifying a general area of interest within the larger framework of European civilization since 1815. Review the course syllabus to be sure you know both the limits and the possibilities for a paper. For instance, in a seminar "European Cultural History, 1880 to 1930," the title sets both topical and chronological limitations; a research paper needs to relate to the subdiscipline called "cultural history." A student would need to ask such questions as "How does cultural history relate to other kinds of history in terms of content and interest?" You always need to select a topic that's important or reaches maturity or full development during the period specified by the title of the course. Consider what you already know about the subject area of the course; think about other courses you've taken, other books and articles you've read, and other papers you've written. Look through and examine journal entries concerning course materials and ideas that particularly interested you, as the relationship between technology and imperialism interests the history student above.

Read what another student has to say about researching and writing a paper that did not fit the criteria for a paper in her seminar "European Cultural History, 1880 to 1930":

> I am somewhat disillusioned with the expectations of the course — but this is really my own fault. I could have known well ahead of time what this course was about and chose not to because I had made up my mind about what I wanted it to be. Because I did not face facts until too late, I was caught short in the rewriting of my paper. . . . I do think that perhaps my experience of failing to

```
accept evident and well presented requirements for
the paper may be of some help to someone else --
although us pigheaded people tend to be immune to
good advice -- preferring to learn the hard way.
```

The student's topic, "The Macedonian Question," dealt with the political and military events leading up to the Balkan Wars of 1912 and 1913 — a topic too remote from cultural history and even more remote from the events of Paris and Vienna that were central to the seminar readings and discussions. And even though the paper was well researched and written, the experience did not contribute much to the student's knowledge of cultural history.

In order that your research and writing experience will add richly to your knowledge of history, you need to be as focused and specific as possible. At this stage, examine the required readings of the course, looking through titles and tables of contents. Reflect on how the readings relate to the course; consider what are and will be the important topics of the course from the readings and their relationships to the syllabus. The best topics are those that relate directly to the course in some way and that are treated, or at least mentioned, in the required readings. Your own academic experience, the course syllabus, the course notebook or journal, and the required readings should be your main sources of inspiration for a paper topic, providing many sound ideas. Best of all, the topics which emerge from these sources will be appropriate.

WRITING 5.3: SELECT A TOPIC BY FOLLOWING INTERESTS. From your course syllabus, required readings, class notes, and journal entries, and your academic interests and background, make a list of possible topics that relate to the course. From this list, select the most interesting topic idea and make a list of everything you already know about it — make your list as exhaustive and as extensive as possible. Your journal would be a good place for this material.

Collecting Material and Focusing Your Interests

Searching the course syllabus, the readings, notes and entries, and your interests should have produced several thoughts about potential topics and perhaps you've even selected one that you think might work for you. After looking over the list or the things you've thought about with regard to one topic idea, pick the most promising one and read everything you can find about that topic in your required readings. Does the topic still seem interesting? Is it too broad? Can you narrow it to a workable area for the length specified by your teacher? Should you change the wording to sharpen the idea?

When you have some general material and ideas about one topic and a list of other potential topics, you may find it helpful to make an appointment with your professor or graduate teaching assistant to discuss your ideas. Or discuss the project with a classmate or friend. What do they think about the topic and about your tentative plans for treating the topic? What is your own point of view toward the topic? What do you think you will find as you do research? What would you like to find out? What would your listener like you to find out about the topic? (These questions might help you more if you wrote about them as we suggest in "your journal as a research log" in Chapters 2 and 6.)

In upper level courses, your professors may be as interested in your research project as you are because they may never have had the opportunity to pursue that topic in any depth and would appreciate learning from your research. Discussing the topic with your teacher and classmates might also give you the benefits of what they know about specific research materials. And discussing your topic and ideas for its development and knowing you are sparking genuine interest in others certainly help make you more enthusiastic.

Student Patricia Tursi narrowed her interest in the broad topic, "the relationships between technology and European imperialism," by focusing on how the discovery of quinine affected European imperialism in Africa in the nineteenth century. Here she explores the idea in a journal entry her teacher assigned, in which she has to discuss her topic by making use of the information in assigned readings. These excerpts show a writer making preliminary connections:

```
April 4, 1986.  The Discovery of Quinine and the
                Penetration of Africa

     Prior to the mid-nineteenth century, the colo-
nization attempts made by Europeans in Africa were
```

futile. Throughout the seventeenth up until the middle of the nineteenth century, tropical disease in Africa made Africa intolerable for Europeans. The diseases which affected Europeans were dysentery, yellow fever, typhoid, and other illnesses, "the principal killer of Europeans in Africa was malaria" (p. 64).

Daniel R. Headrick, in his book <u>The Tools of Empire</u>, gives detailed accounts of the devastation which malaria produced among Europeans; for example, during the year of 1824 224 British soldiers were sent to Africa and 221 lost their lives due to disease. . . . average 77% of the white soldiers sent to West Africa perished. It is for this reason that Africa became known as the "white man's grave" (p. 64).

It is obvious that colonization of Africa was impossible and undesirable. So the Europeans turned their attention to other areas of the world such as the Americas. Yet throughout the seventeenth and eighteenth centuries, Europeans carried on coastal trade with Africa. During this time, experiments were done using the bark of the cinchona tree which held the alkaloid quinine. But it was not until 1820 when two French scientists discovered how to extract quinine from the cinchona bark. It is at this point that quinine became manufactured in large enough quantities for general use. . . . British and French doctors began to prescribe quinine to the men who were a part of exploring expeditions on steamers, another product of technology. After various experientation and observations of the effects of quinine connected with the treatment of malaria, most notably Macgregor Laird's expedition on the Pleid River, was the value of quinine totally realized.

By using quinine as a prophylactic, the frontiers of Africa became tolerable for Europeans. The ramifications of the use of this new drug were enormous, for it allowed Europeans of the mid-nineteenth century to penetrate the interior of Africa. . . . . With the use of quinine Africa was no longer regarded as the "white man's grave" but was regarded as an area of the world which would be useful for European desires.

Notice how much specific information Patricia Tursi was able to find about the needs for and early development of quinine with reference to class texts, especially Headrick's book. She's also able to gloss over early experiments, knowing she'll go into detail later when she's able to fill in from her research. Writing about what you already know about your topic and what you can find in your texts can give you a good "feel" for what you will need to do at the outset.

Also you assert your own control from the beginning with this early working knowledge as a basis for further research.

> WRITING 5.4: WRITING WHAT YOU KNOW. In a journal entry, write everything you already know about your topic and any information you can find in your readings. What's important here is the quantity of detailed information you can come up with. Also, be sure to consult the lists you made in an earlier journal entry.

Before the Library

At this point, you have a clear understanding of the context for the paper; you have identified a likely and workable topic; you have read about that topic in the course readings; you have written about what you've read; and you have discussed your tentative plans with an interested person. You are nearly ready to begin your library research, but before you do, read all of Chapter 6, *Principles of Library Research and Basic Bibliographies.* There we show you research strategies to make your library time more efficient and more effective.

> WRITING 5.5: MAKING A BIBLIOGRAPHY. Look over your texts and, in your journal, make a list of any pertinent references (both books and articles by author and title) you find at the ends of chapters or at the back of books as endnotes. Take these with you to the library as the beginnings of a bibliography.

HANDLING AND ORGANIZING YOUR RESEARCH

Your campus library will almost always have more than enough information available on your topic if you go about your research in the most productive ways. The question is more often, "What do I do with **all** this material?" Organization becomes the key.

If you are not prone to be systematic, now is the time to mend your habits — if not for your whole college career, at least reform for the duration of this research project. First, there is no way to get around reading the material your research turns up; there is, also, no way you can read enough research material for writing a paper and remember what you've read without taking notes. For the purposes of writing a history research paper, reading without taking notes just wastes your valuable time.

But, you may ask, what kind of notes? How do you know what to write down? What should you write your notes on?

Bibliography Cards and Note Cards

The first thing you should do after finding a promising book or article in the card catalogue is to make a **bibliography** or **"bib" card** on that source. Bib cards with all the information **correctly** recorded will save you tremendous amounts of aggravation and time later on. In a way, your bib cards are the heart of your research effort, because you will use them as the basis for the organization of your note cards and as the record of the information necessary to make proper and accurate endnote citations.

Bib cards are standard sized index cards, 3″ × 5″. They will serve as records of the books and articles you use. You will need the author, title, publication information, and date. (See Chapter 7, *Documentation Techniques,* for bibliographic citation form.) It also helps to record your library's call number of the book or periodical in case you need to find that source again. Make a brief note to yourself on other valuable features of the source such as "good photographs," or "statistical tables in the appendixes," or "excellent maps." These remarks will be exactly what you need if your teacher requires that you annotate your bibliography or that you write a bibliographic essay evaluating your sources. (See information about annotated bibliographies and bibliographic essays in Chapter 7, *Documentation Techniques.*)

Headrick, Daniel R.

The Tools of Empire: Technology and European Imperialism in the Nineteenth Century.

New York: Oxford University Press, 1981.
(Has an excellent bibliography.)

Figure 5.1 *Sample bibliography card.*

These bib cards are crucial for this research project, of course, but since you will be writing many papers in college, especially if you are a history major, you should save them for future use. The best file is a small metal box (fireproof), with alphabetical spacers especially designed for index cards. Graduate students and professors take their bibliographic files along when they travel to other research libraries. Someday your cards will begin to look used, perhaps with different call number entries representing the various libraries and different cataloging systems — something like a well-traveled passport.

Armed with bibliography cards and some books and articles, you need to begin the reading/note-taking process. There are a number of comprehension strategies that can help you as you read the material you've collected.

- Skim the material first to get a general idea of what it contains. Pay special attention to first paragraphs, first sentences in paragraphs, and to conclusions.
- Be alert as you read so you can go back quickly to catch up and understand if you miss a point or get confused.
- If you cannot follow the gist of the author's argument, stop

reading and think about the material. Write about what you don't understand. Formulate questions.

- If the material is difficult, try to restate the main points and ideas every few pages or paragraphs. Summarize the main ideas and then write your own summary as your notes.

You need to be an active reader to become a good researcher. These strategies should get you pointed in the right direction. More importantly, you will have the essential information written down in your own words, ready to recall and use in writing your paper.

Use **note cards** as you take these notes on the reading. Their size is up to you as long as they are uniform in size. The 4″ × 6″ cards seem most popular with the 5½″ × 8″ a close second. Be sure that each note card has the source and page number(s) specifically identified. You can develop your own shorthand identification for the source, based on your bib card. The trick is to identify your source on the note card so that you can relate it directly to the bib card for the complete information. This short identification must appear on every note card you write. Put the identification of your source with page number of the noted information on the top of the card.

Figure 5.2 (opposite) shows how a note card might look.

Identification which keys your note cards to your bib cards is especially important for any quotations and paraphrasing you do of the source material. Nothing makes you more frustrated or takes so much time than wanting to use a quotation and finding that you forgot to record the source and page number. If you do not have this information and cannot recover it, you cannot use the quotation, no matter how wonderfully apt it is.

Extracting quotations from your source material requires special care. Be sure to enclose all direct quotes, so that three or four days later you can distinguish the quote from your own notes. Copy the quotation exactly as it appears in the source, with every punctuation mark and spelling feature. If you decide to quote only a portion of the passage, indicate where you have left out material with an ellipsis — three dots, spaced apart (. . .) if omitted material is from within a sentence — four dots (. . . .) if the omitted material

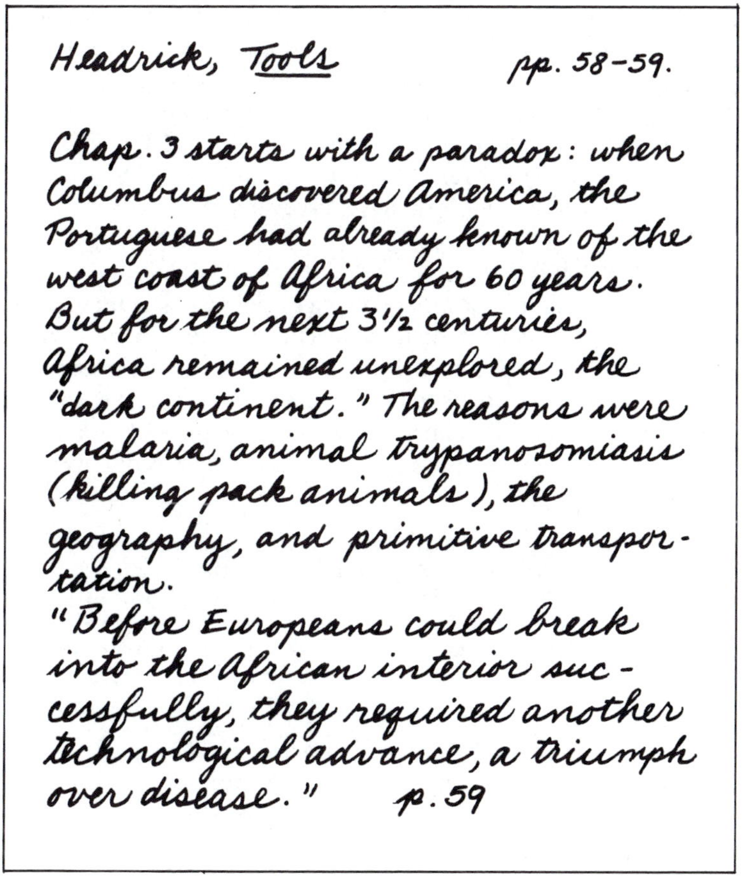

Headrick, Tools pp. 58–59.

Chap. 3 starts with a paradox: when Columbus discovered America, the Portuguese had already known of the west coast of Africa for 60 years. But for the next 3½ centuries, Africa remained unexplored, the "dark continent." The reasons were malaria, animal trypanosomiasis (killing pack animals), the geography, and primitive transportation.
"Before Europeans could break into the African interior successfully, they required another technological advance, a triumph over disease." p. 59

Figure 5.2 *Sample note card.*

covers more than a sentence. If you need to add material within the quotation, do so with brackets [ ], not parentheses.

Keep all notecards on the same source together with a rubber band for each packet. Only when you have a plan for your paper will you want to break up your packets and arrange them by subject matter.

WRITING 5.6: DOING LIBRARY RESEARCH. Locate as many primary and secondary sources as you need (at least one primary source and at least three secondary sources), and make bib cards and note cards. After reading and taking notes, write a research log entry on your topic at this stage. Has your hypothesis or thesis changed or become modified? What is the most interesting thing you have discovered?

Generating Material

Looking at topics from a variety of angles can stimulate interesting, more original ways of making connections. (Refer to the section *Organized Questioning* in Chapter 3.) In the following journal entry, Patricia Tursi responds to an assignment requesting her to look at her topic through its connection with something else; she considers the importance of European technology to the discovery of quinine:

> There is one innovation of European technology, which grew out of industrialism, which is of vital importance in how it relates to the discovery and use of quinine as a preventive medicine against malaria. The innovation which I think is of extreme importance was the internal combustion engine and the use of steel to produce steamships. Without the development of the steamer, the application of quinine would not have had as great an impact. With this new mode of transportation, Europeans were able to explore other parts of the world, such as Africa, with more efficiency.
>
> Even prior to the use of quinine, steamers were used to explore rivers in Africa. These two developments are extremely interrelated and I must try to sort them out. Without steamers the interior rivers of Africa would not have been explored. The exploration of rivers in Africa led to the observations that disease made these efforts futile. As a result, various experimentations for the treatment of tropical diseases, especially malaria, were undertaken upon the steamers which navigated the rivers of the area. Trial and error led to an effective treatment against the diseases which had kept Europeans out of Africa. Therefore making coloniza-

tion possible. The use of steamers and the administration of quinine among the crews of the steamers used for exploration, were two technological developments that helped new imperialism.

These two technological developments must be placed within the broader scheme of Europe's new imperialism. As Palmer points out, "Imperialism arose from the commercial, industrial, financial, scientific, political, journalistic, intellectual, religious, and humanitarian impulses of Europe compounded together" (pp. 615-616).

Here, Patricia Tursi is making what look like some important associations and connections that will make her paper more substantial. She is in the process of seeing how her topic is part of a rich body of material that cannot be ignored.

WRITING 5.7: WAYS OF SEEING. Write a journal entry in which you examine your topic through its connections with something else. Does this writing generate additional material, ways of seeing that add to how you might treat your topic?

Creating Context

At this stage in your research process, it may give some added perspective if you consider your topic within a larger context or from a different perspective. Student Patricia Tursi's teacher asked that students write about their topics in their journals within the appropriate broader context; for her that meant quinine in the broader context of the new imperialism:

With the discovery and the use of quinine in the treatment of malaria and as a preventative for the fever, the climate of Africa became tolerable for Europeans. The result was that Europeans were now able to explore and to penetrate the African continent. Even when quinine was used as just a treatment during exploration expeditions, it allowed Europeans to take a look at the interior of Africa. The use of quinine also stimulated the development of more missionary efforts in Africa. Within my paper, I do not want to spend a great deal of time describing Europeans' new Imperialism.

> The major point I want to make is that quinine made it a reality. Also, I would like to argue that the discovery of quinine was a characteristic of the new Imperialism, due to the fact that it was a scientific discovery which was made possible by the changes which occurred in Europe due to Industrialism. I guess also I would have to speak briefly of why Europeans wanted to extend themselves. (What were their desires?) Why was Africa attractive to them? Africa's attraction is due to the discovery of quinine. So quinine partly was as much a result of the new Imperialism and Industrialism as it was a factor in stimulating the new Imperialism. The discovery of quinine grew out of European efforts to extend themselves and it allowed Europeans to extend themselves. This is a really jumbled journal entry.

Notice how Tursi's sentences become tangled and more complex as she is in the process of modifying and clarifying her thesis. This writing to the self has value at this stage of synthesizing and assimilating sources. This entry is less smooth than the earlier one based on less knowledge and material, a good sign that the writer is wrestling with complicated material and greater amounts of evidence. She ended knowing certain things she doesn't want to do, as well as getting on track about what she does see her research leading her toward.

WRITING 5.8: MORE WAYS OF SEEING. Write a journal entry in which you examine your topic within its larger context. What happened? What did you find out? Can you locate a potential thesis?

WRITING YOUR PAPER

Planning

With a sound feel for the resources and having examined a topic in a variety of ways, you should be ready to develop a working plan for the organization and presentation of your research paper. A plan may alert you to weak spots in your research. Patricia Tursi made her plan in the form of an outline; she was probably better able to come up with a sound organizational plan at the outset because of the prewriting she had done:

Plan for Paper

I Introduction -- thesis

II Early attempts of European penetration into Africa

  A. Problems of disease

  B. Case examples

  C. Attitude which developed toward Africa

III Industrialism

  A. Changes attitudes

  B. Provides new motives and incentives for exploring Africa

  C. Results in New Imperialism

IV 19th-century attempts to explore Africa

  A. Laird

  B. Trotter

  C. French case

V Discovery of quinine

  A. Evolution of discovery

  B. Experimentation & observation concerning new drug

    1. Livingstone

    2. Meller

  C. Lack of scientific knowledge

VI Conclusion

VII Appendix

A. 4 personal journal entries

B. Rough draft

C. 3 professional journal articles (primary sources)

D. Map of African rivers?

WRITING 5.9: WRITING A PLAN. Your written plan may be an outline or a series of sentences or phrases, whatever works best for you. If you do an outline, you might find it strengthens the plan if you write out your thesis in one or two sentences. Was it hard to make a plan? easy?

The Prewriting Process

Writing this research paper requires using journal entries as the vehicle for prewriting and you may find yourself returning to your journal to try passages out as you continue with a draft of the entire paper. But even if you do not keep a class journal, we strongly urge you to consider doing entries for your paper, similar to the ones above, as informal pieces of writing. But why should you bother with all this prewriting before drafting the paper? Read what Patricia Tursi had to say in her journal research log about the value of the prewriting process as she wrote her paper:

2/24/86 #13 A Note On the Paper

I have never done a paper in this manner. I found by doing previous journal entries, my thoughts and ideas concerning the topic I chose to write about were clearer. It gave me a starting base when I usually do not start with one. I found that it involved me in my topic without worrying about form or word choice and this made it easier to construct an effective outline. Once I began to write the body of my paper, I enjoyed it more because if I became blocked for ideas, I was able to refer to my journal entries and an idea on how I would want to continue would spark. I have found that this process is an effective technique to use when beginning a paper. I look forward to applying the new method to other history papers this semester and in my future college career.

Drafting to Discover and Revising to Clarify

No accomplished writer writes anything once and finds it entirely satisfactory. Or, if it should happen, the occasion is as memorable as Keats's description of composing "On First Looking into Chapman's Homer" as he walked home through the early morning streets of London. Most often the one-shot wonder piece is simplistic, incomplete, or both.

Sometimes the writer needs to begin to write a piece to see where it will go and how it will look — much as E. H. Carr describes his itch to write in the conclusion of Chapter 3 — "I begin to write — not necessarily at the beginning, but somewhere, anywhere." Writers need to ask questions of their prose. Are the ideas well developed? Do they hang together? Is my point well supported? Did my argument work out? Do I need to say more? or less?

The draft is where the interaction between research and writing occurs. Historian Carr refers to this interrelationship in Chapter 3 and so does the student author earlier in this chapter. The draft is where you shape the paper and begin to conceive it as a whole piece — to see what it looks like. The original outline or plan is bound to undergo changes and emendation as you write. If we are ever required to produce a clean outline, it has to be written after completing the final copy, not before. Writers of books know only too well that the table of contents comes after the manuscript is finished, after it has taken its final shape.

Whether you do a tentative outline or a journal description of your plan or a detailed outline, you need some organizational scheme to follow that gives you a wedge into your material. Your plan, whatever it is, enables you to organize your note cards and arrange them according to plan. These groupings provide the evidence and the quotations for each of the parts of your draft. The easiest way to do this reshuffling is on a large, clean surface, your desk or the kitchen table. Triple-space your draft at the outset, whether you compose directly on the keyboard or in a handwritten script. This practice makes revision easier.

Since revision means "seeing again, viewing in a different way," you must have a written draft to work from. The revision process is one of the most powerful learning opportunities you have. You see what you have created; you appreciate what you have produced after hours of reading, researching, and writing. Now you want to make it better. Remember not to worry about the fine-tuning of mechanics; you are still after ideas, organization, and effectiveness. Write another beginning; sharpen the lead to make it more interesting. Try for another kind of conclusion than a summary of main points. Is there an especially powerful quote that you could use to pull your ideas together in a more effective meshing in the final part of your paper? Reread pages three and four; put them aside and try to write them differently. After all, this paper does represent a lot of yourself and you want to do yourself full justice.

Reading Your Paper to Yourself and Others

Your revised draft can serve as the basis for sharing your work in the peer review process described in Chapter 3, *Approaches to Writing and Learning History.* Patricia Tursi had a classmate read her paper and even though her revision process was well along, her reader made insightful and invaluable suggestions, such as "would like better descriptions of the diseases and further explanation of social Darwinism and white man's burden." And this list gets even more specific:

1. On p. 3, the second paragraph — "One of the tech . . . ," relate it more to the discovery of quinine as a cure;
2. Maybe you could put this paragraph at the beginning of the paper — shocking readers with these statistics, capturing their attention immediately;
3. A little more information on the effects (Headrick).

Whether or not you take all suggestions, getting a reader's reaction helps you see your own prose differently. Peer review gives you the chance to get away from your paper for a while as well as the opportunity to get a little help from your friends. They will, of course, be able to be most responsive if they have a neatly typed draft to read.

Patricia Tursi expresses the value of the peer review process in her journal:

> "I found this review to be beneficial. I found myself involved in the other person's writing and I gained satisfaction from helping an individual improve this skill."

Seeing what you wrote in this draft helps revision. So does hearing your paper in your own voice or read aloud by a friend. Actually professional meetings — formal meetings of all types — require oral presentations of papers before an audience. Reading your paper aloud to a friend gives you a chance to evaluate the sound of your prose and to make it sound more pleasing and more substantial.

> WRITING 5.10: DRAFTING AND REVISING. Write a draft of your paper from written plans developed in Writing 5.9 and prewriting materials gathered in Writings 5.5–5.8. Revise as many times as you need to over a period of at least a week if possible. Have a classmate read your paper for specific areas that are giving you trouble.

Editing to Share Knowledge

Recently *The New York Times* came out against an important judicial appointment because the candidate lacked experience and could not express himself effectively within the conventions of standard American English. Finishing touches matter. The final draft of your essay represents you as historian. Editing means putting the final touches on the manuscript to eliminate errors of diction, grammar, and punctuation.

But the most important reason to give your prose the finishing touches is that it is a piece of history. Your interpretation of the sources, your point of view toward the topic, your emphases, and your supported hypotheses make this work unique. There has never been a historical account exactly like yours and there never will be again. Limitations of resources and time may not have allowed you to discover new primary sources, but you have made a contribution by writing a piece of history. You have made the topic your own, given it your interpretation. Since the manuscript represents you, it should be as perfect as it can be for your readers — classmates, interested friends, and your professor. Consult Chapter 7, *Documentation Techniques,* Chapter 8, *A Concise Guide to Usage,* and Chapter 9, *Make Punctuation Work for You,* for practical references during the editing stage.

WRITING 5.11: EDITING. Read Chapters 8 and 9 on usage and punctuation. Before typing the final copy of your research paper, check the prose for any surface errors. Check the endnotes and bibliography for accuracy of form and content. Read backward and read aloud so that no errors slip through. Have a good friend read the paper aloud. Even if you find on the day the paper's due that a sentence has a misplaced phrase or clause, it's always permissible to mark through and to make necessary editing changes neatly printed in black ink.

Here is the way Patricia Tursi's paper turned out:

Quinine and Europe's New Imperialism:

A Result as Well as a Cause

Patricia Tursi

Professor Steffens

History 6

April 18, 1986

At the end of the nineteenth century, European powers began to penetrate the interior of Africa. During this era, European powers, particularly the British and the French, implemented aggressive expansionist policies which have been termed by historians as the new imperialism of Europe. A variety of factors, which stem from the advancement of European culture, contributed to the rise of Europe's new imperialism. The historian R.R. Palmer precisely illustrates that Europe's new imperialism "arose from the commercial, industrial, financial, scientific, political, journalistic, intellectual, religious, and humanitarian impulses of Europe compounded together."[1] Within this broad spectrum of factors which contributed to European motives to penetrate Africa, this essay will concentrate upon a small but vital aspect of technology which resulted in the scientific discovery of the drug quinine. The discovery and the use of quinine can be viewed as a result as well as a cause of Europe's new imperialism.[2]

Prior to the middle of the nineteenth century, the attempts made by Europeans to pierce the remote continent of Africa were futile. Throughout the

2

seventeenth, the eighteenth, and the early nineteenth centuries, disease plagued European explorers, leaving Africa an unmapped area of the world. Europeans were unable to resist the afflictions of dysentery, yellow fever, typhoid, and other tropical illnesses. The one disease which was the primary obstacle to European endeavors in Africa was malaria. This disease is recognized by periodic chills and fever, anemia, general poor health, and an enlarged spleen. Malaria was the principal killer of Europeans and it made Africa intolerable for them.[3] Daniel Headrick, in The Tools of Empire, lists the appalling death rates of a few early European ventures:

> . . . in 1777–79, during William Bolts' expedition at Delagoa Bay, 132 out of 152 Europeans on the journey died. Mungo Park's 1805 venture to the upper Niger resulted in death of all the Europeans present.[4]

Due to the calamitous results of early expeditionary forces, Europeans perceived Africa as the "dark continent" and regarded this area of the world as the "white man's grave."[5] European indifference towards Africa led to the expansion and the settlement of the Americas, Asia, and Australia during the first era of imperialism.[6]

The nineteenth century ushered in the age of industrialism in Europe. Industrialism produced profound changes in societal attitudes concerning the perceived need to explore the "dark continent."[7] These ideas, which arose out of the advancement of European culture, generated new rationalizations for expansion, which were based upon missionary, economic, nationalistic, and strategic justifications. Prior to the nineteenth century, missionary efforts did exist in Africa. But due to the change brought about by industrialism, the missionary effort of Europeans during the nineteenth century began to employ the notions of Social Darwinism and the concept of the White Man's Burden. Social Darwinism and the White Man's Burden were both racist ideologies held by Europeans of the nineteenth century; these ideologies were used as a justification for imperialism and the havoc which imperialism wrought upon indigenous peoples. The economic motives behind European expansion also shifted, as the merchant class of industrialized

4

European nations perceived the need for creating new markets for their manufactured goods and the necessity of obtaining supplies of raw materials. During this era of intellectual change, Europeans began to identify national honor with the size of a country's colonial holdings. And with the growth in the use of steamships in European navies, colonial holdings were also viewed as strategically important. Africa, which was a remote and unmapped continent, became a prime candidate for European expansion and by the mid-nineteenth century Europeans had the technology needed to carry out their desires.

One of the technological developments vital to the exploration of Africa was the steamboat. Steamers were used extensively in mid-nineteenth century ventures carried out by Europeans in Africa. Even though the development of the steamer overcame the obstacle of transportation, Europeans were unable to break into the interior of the continent successfully, due to the problems of disease. Headrick points out that Europeans "required another technological advance, a triumph over disease."[8]

In 1832, an Englishman, Macgregor Laird, who

embodied the new attitudes which Europeans held, organized an expedition to Niger using the steamers the "Quorra" and the "Albrukah." The size of the crew on the "Quorra" was 26 men and the "Albrukah" crew consisted of 14 men. Both of these vessels entered the Nan branch of the Niger on October 18, 1832. Upon immediate entrance onto the river, members of the crews on both vessels encountered the miserable disease of malaria. By November 14, 1832, only one European on the "Quorra" was fit for active duty. By November 21, 1832, the crew of the "Quorra" was decreased by the death of 13 men and the "Albrukah" had lost two. By 1833, both of these vessels withdrew from the river, forced to return to the open sea due to the deplorable conditions disease had produced. The expedition ended in total failure, resulting in 24 deaths on the "Quorra" and 15 deaths on the "Albrukah."[9]

The above scenario was not uncommon; throughout the first half of the nineteenth century many other expeditions met the same fate. Captain Trotter's expedition on the Niger in the years of 1841-42, using the steamers "Albert," "Wilberforce," and "Soudan," was paralyzed by the effects which malaria wracked upon the crews.[10] The French met equal disaster following their invasion of Algeria in the 1830's.[11]

Even though these attempts to penetrate the interior of Africa were distressing failures, in the eyes of Europeans they were not unfruitful failures. Doctors who accompanied these expeditions began the struggle of experimentation and observation in order to discover a cure to the disease which was blocking European expansion, malaria. As Headrick reveals, the fact that

> the cause of malaria was not known to science until the end of the century did not prevent a remedy from emerging much earlier out of a long process of trial and error. Before our own century, technological advances often preceded a scientific explanation of the underlying natural phenomena.[12]

This process of trial and error is evident in the history surrounding the discovery of a cure for malaria. In the seventeenth century, the Jesuits introduced the use of the bark of the cinchona tree as a cure for vivax malaria. In the eighteenth century, medical authorities began to regularly prescribe this bark as a remedy for the fever. But a breakthrough did not occur until the 1820's when two French chemists, Pierre Joseph Pelletier and Joseph Bienaimé Caventour were successful in extracting the alkaloid of quinine from the cinchona bark. By 1827 commercial production of quinine began and by 1830 the drug was being manufactured in large enough quantities for general use.[13] It is interesting to note that by the time that the alkaloid of quinine was discovered, Europeans had the ability to produce the drug commercially. It is equally important to realize that the discovery of this drug grew out of the demand to find an effective combatant against malaria in order to penetrate Africa. In this perspective, the discovery of quinine can be seen as a consequence of Europe's new imperialism.

Even though quinine was discovered by the nineteenth century, Europeans lacked the ability to identify the way in which the disease was transmitted and they also lacked the ability to distinguish between the two strains of the disease. Headrick provides a pithy description of the two varieties of the disease:

> Tertian malaria, endemic throughout much of the world, is caused by the protozoan Plasmodium vivax and produces intermittent fevers and a general weakening of the body. Another variety, brought on by the Plasmodium falciparum, is endemic only to tropical Africa and is far deadlier.[14]

As a result of the lack of this scientific knowledge in the nineteenth century, the administration of quinine as an effective remedy against the two strains of malaria had to undergo its own process of trial and error.

By the mid-1840's, Europeans began to regularly take quinine at the first signs of the fever. This treatment was a successful agent against the vivax form of malaria but it proved to be insufficient against the falciparum form. In order for quinine to be effective against the falciparum strain, it had to be used as a prophylactic.[15]

By the middle of the nineteenth century, quinine began to be used extensively by Europeans. One explorer, David Livingstone, heard about quinine and used the drug during his march across Southern Africa from 1850 to 1856:

> In 1850 I (D. Livingstone) adopted the plan of giving quinine mixed with a purgative as the first step of the treatment, and was successful. I have been successful in every case I have met.[16]

Here is David Livingstone's recipe:

> resin of jalap and colomel, of each eight grains; quinine and rhubarb, of each four grains; mix well together, and when required make into pills with spirit of cardomons; dose from ten to twenty grains.[17]

This prescription has become known as the "Livingstone Pill." Even though this explorer was successful with his experimentations involving quinine, he concluded that the drug was not effective as a preventive against the disease.[18]

Another explorer, Charles J. Meller, who was the "surgeon-naturalist in medical charge" for several expeditions off the South-East coast of Africa

10

and in East Central Africa, also experimented with quinine.[19] When Meller returned from Africa to Europe, he published his observations concerning the use of quinine during an expedition in 1861 which was "spent in the Rovuma, Zambesi and Shire rivers" in the British Medical Journal.[20] His journal article explicitly describes the problem of disease which this venture encountered and the way in which he administered quinine. Like Livingstone, Meller used quinine as treatment only after the symptoms of the fever became apparent. Meller's observations and accounts were insightful for the era and were a part of the long process of trial and error but they lacked a true scientific understanding of malaria. In both of the expeditions which he was involved in, he found quinine to be an insufficient drug against malaria.

After an assessment of Livingstone's and Meller's writing, it is apparent that both men lacked the ability to distinguish between the two strains of malaria. Livingstone's description of the fever he encountered depicts the symptoms of the vivax strain; this strain has a regular two-day fever cycle. His observations concluded that quinine was a successful agent against malaria. Yet Meller's description of the fever he encountered correlates with the symptoms of the more fatal strain falciparum. This strain has an irregular cycle, and fever may be more or less continuous, with chills and sweating at irregular intervals. His observations led him to conclude that quinine was an inadequate drug. Due to the inability of Europeans to distinguish between the two different types of malaria, the most effective treatment, using quinine as a prophylactic, was not administered to men who were in the clutches of the fatal falciparum strain. As a result, Europeans continued to suffer from this form of malaria in Africa. It is interesting to note that Meller observed that "the excessive irritation from mosquito bites will keep up fever, in spite of all treatment."[21] But it was not discovered until the end of the nineteenth century that the mosquito transmitted the disease.[22]

Africa remained a hostile place to the health of many Europeans because they did not fully understand the nature and the treatment of malaria. But with the discovery of quinine, there was an improvement. The Europeans who were afflicted with

12

vivax malaria and treated with quinine were surviving; this resulted in a decrease of the mortality rate. As the use of quinine spread, the mortality rates fell from 65 per 1,000 in 1825–45 to 22 per 1,000 in 1858–67. By the late nineteenth century, "the first-year death rates among Europeans in West Africa dropped from 250–750 per 1,000 to 50–100 per 1,000."[23] As the death rate continued to decrease, Europeans no longer looked upon Africa as the "white man's grave." The use of quinine made the climate of Africa tolerable for European existence. "River steamers had overcome the obstacle of poor transportation and quinine that of malaria. Together, they opened much of Africa to colonialism."[24]

13

ENDNOTES

[1]R.R. Palmer and Joel Colton. A History of the Modern World Since 1815(New York: Alfred A. Knopf, 1984), 615–16.

[2]Daniel R. Headrick, The Tools of Empire(New York: Oxford University Press, 1981), 73.

[3]Headrick, 64.

[4]Headrick, 59–60.

[5]Headrick, 58 and 64.

[6]Headrick, 58.

[7]Headrick, 58.

[8]Headrick, 59.

[9]David Livingstone, "On fever in the Zambesi: A note from Dr. Livingstone to Dr. M'William." Lancet, August 24, 1861, in Micheal Gelfand, Living-

stone the Doctor(Oxford: Basil Blackwell, 1957), 300.

[10]Livingstone, 301.

[11]Headrick, 66.

[12]Headrick, 65.

[13]Headrick, 65-66.

[14]Headrick, 64.

[15]Headrick, 67.

[16]Livingstone, 297.

[17]Livingstone, 297.

[18]Livingstone, 297.

[19]Charles J. Meller, "On the Fever of East Central Africa." Lancet. October 22, 1864 in Micheal Gel-

fand, Livingstone the Doctor(Oxford: Basil Blackwell, 1957), 312.

[20]Charles James Meller, "Fevers of the South-East Coast of Africa." British Medical Journal. October 25, 1862 in Micheal Gelfand, Livingstone the Doctor(Oxford: Basil Blackwell, 1957), 304.

[21]Meller, British Medical Journal, 310.

[22]Headrick, 78.

[23]Headrick, 70.

[24]Headrick, 73.

16

BIBLIOGRAPHY

Headrick, Daniel R. The Tools of Empire. New York: Oxford University Press, 1981. Very Helpful. Provides an insightful analysis concerning the importance of European technological advancement and how the development of European technology contributed to the rise of Europe's new imperialism. Devotes an entire chapter to the discovery and the use of quinine against malaria which was extremely well researched.

Livingstone, David. "On Fever in the Zambesi: A note from Dr. Livingstone to Dr. M'William." Lancet. August 24, 1861, in Micheal Gelfand, Livingstone the Doctor. Oxford: Basil Blackwell, 1957. Provides a firsthand account of the use of quinine in an African expedition. Gives a detailed description of the type of treatment used and the type of fever encountered. Provides case studies concerning early attempts of the penetration of Africa by Europeans. Helpful.

Meller, Charles James. "Fevers of the South-East Coast of Africa." British Medical Journal. October 25, 1862, in Micheal Gelfand, Livingstone the Doctor. Oxford: Basil Blackwell, 1957. Provides first-hand observations concerning the use of quinine against malaria in Africa. Stresses the insufficiency of quinine against the type of fever which was encountered. Helpful.

Meller, Charles J. "On the Fever of East Central Africa." Lancet. October 22, 1864 in Micheal Gelfand, Livingstone the Doctor. Oxford: Basil Blackwell, 1957. Stresses previous conclusions published in the British Medical Journal article combined with case studies of individuals which suffered from malaria and underwent treatment which included the administration of quinine in Africa. Assumes that a better prophylactic than quinine exists in the use of stimulus.

Palmer, R.R. and Joel Colton. A History of the Modern World Since 1815. New York: Alfred A. Knopf, 1984. Standard European history textbook to be used for introductory history courses on the university level. Provides necessary background information on European history.

FURTHER THOUGHTS ON WRITING HISTORY
Marguerite Yourcenar's "Reflections on the Composition of the Memoirs of Hadrian"*

Marguerite Yourcenar recommends that history researchers totally immerse themselves in their subjects, almost to the point of becoming another person, in another time and place: "learn everything, read everything, inquire into everything, . . . try to visualize ever more exactly the images which they create beneath their closed eyelids." She goes on to urge that we pursue each incident "Through hundreds of note cards . . . to the very moment that it occurred; . . . . read a text of the Second Century with the eyes, soul, and feelings of the Second Century. . . ." Yet while advising us to keep our own "shadow[s] out of the picture; leave the mirror clean of the mist of one's own breath," she tells us to make honest and full use "of all possibilities for comparison and cross-checking, and of new perspectives slowly developed by the many centuries and events separating us from a given text, a fact, a man. . . ."

What writing history makes possible, though, is our entry into another time, another culture, and another's life or, as Yourcenar puts it, "our point of contact with those . . . who, like us, nibbled olives and drank wine, or gummed their fingers with honey . . . who took their pleasures, thought their own thoughts, grew old, and died." Writing history from extensive research inserts our texts, like Yourcenar's, into the larger ongoing discourse of history.

**Memoirs of Hadrian*. New York: Farrar, Straus and Giroux, 1954. 330–331.

[6] *Principles of Library Research and Basic Bibliographies*

PREVIEW: *One of the greatest indirect aids to the success of your research is how comfortable and welcome you feel in your campus library. Our aim in this chapter is to show you how to conduct research so that you learn to make the most of your library's resources and your own resources.*

The most important part of any educational experience is the learning that you initiate yourself. Here is what Molly Wickes wrote in her research log about doing a research paper:

> What was exciting in all of this was how much I actually learned. My topic turned out to be a really exciting one and kept my interest and dedication throughout the many pains of writing a research paper. What was interesting was that just the process of reading and skimming books and writing notecards led me to form opinions regarding my topic which differed to some degree from other historians on the subject. After learning about the topic I found I could write about it in an intelligent, historical manner. Other things which I learned and other opinions I hold all related to the way I internalized my topic. I made connections about events and ideas which other historians didn't. My actual paper grew out of my work as an original historian which is something I didn't really realize until I viewed the final draft. I still feel that I have a lot of work to do on my paper. For the time being it's done but I know that sometime in my life I'm going to have to pursue all those points that I left out of my final draft.

Our aim in this chapter is to show you how to conduct research so that you experience this intellectual excitement. To do that, you need to learn how to make the most of your library's resources and your own resources.

THE LIBRARY

One of the greatest indirect aids to the success of your research is how comfortable and welcome you feel in your campus library. It should be familiar to you, a place in which you know where things are and a place where you feel everything is waiting to help you. But your initial response to the library was probably anything but enthusiastic. It might have been very much like sitting in front of a computer screen for the first time. "What do I do now? How does this thing work? How do I begin? I don't really want to do this!"

The best way to lose "libraryphobia," as well as "computerphobia," is to USE both yourself. You may not need a special guided tour to begin. Be adventurous and go to each part of the library by yourself. Take some time and explore. Go everywhere and see everything; stop in the middle of a row of book stacks and see what is there; pull a bound volume of a periodical off the shelf and leaf through it; look at how many newspapers from all over the world your library subscribes to; go to every floor and to every corner of every floor. Did you know that your library has a map collection? Do you wonder what is in the microfilm collection? Glance at the display cases and at the artwork on the walls. Librarians take special pride in making the library interesting and attractive. Plan to go back and take a better look at the displays when you need a study break. In addition to getting to know the library, you will probably turn up nooks and crannies that are good places to study when you need a really secluded spot.

Even if your library has closed stacks, there is plenty to discover and explore. Find the **circulation desk,** where books and other materials are checked in and out of the library. The **reserve desk** is the place where professors place reading materials to supplement the required readings. These materials will appear on the reading assignments section of your course syllabus. The **periodicals section** contains current issues of newspapers and magazines, as well as scholarly journals. The issues for the current year are usually shelved in this section. Periodicals for previous years are bound together and placed in the stacks; newspapers are usually stored on microfilm.

The **microfilm section** has the equipment to allow you to read the microfilms, as well as the microfilm collection itself. As the number of periodicals continues to grow and as library storage space continues to fill up, more periodicals must be stored on microfilm. Sooner or later you will be using the microfilm section of your library.

In the **reference section,** you will find much of the material that we introduce in this chapter: abstracts, atlases, bibliographies, books-in-print catalogues, dictionaries, encyclopedias, and indexes. Best of all, this section has the reference librarian. No one can be more helpful or save you more time and frustration than your reference librarian. Take exploration of the library seriously. Some people spend four years on campus and never find half of what the library has to offer. Too bad, especially after paying library fees. It is your library, waiting for you to use it. Also, most professions and many jobs after graduation will assume that you have attained the basic library research skills. Knowing how to do library research will help you advance in your chosen job or profession.

STARTING YOUR RESEARCH AT HOME

Your research should be already well under way before you set foot in the library. In Chapter 5 you looked through books on the required reading list to find a topic. All of these books have bibliographies where you start your research. These bibliographies are valuable for two kinds of sources: (1) specific titles and authors of books and articles related to your topic; and (2) a beginning list of history journals which publish articles related to your topic. The *Journal of the History of Ideas* would be a good source for articles on a topic in intellectual history, for example, but not on military history. Making a list of journals that deal with articles related to your topic gets you started on your research.

Of course, you will begin by making out a bibliography card for each source you think will be useful. Your bib. card should contain all of the necessary information for your later bibliography. (See Chapter 5 for details.) You might as well fill the card out right the first time, instead of jotting down incomplete references on random scraps of paper. Take these bib. cards to the library, look up the sources in the card catalogue, note the call numbers on the bib. cards, get the sources, and your research has begun. This sounds easy, and it really is.

CARD CATALOGUE

Library research almost always begins with the card catalogue. (If your library has computerized its catalogue, you'll find that the following explanation still applies.) If you are looking for a specific title, each book that the library owns is represented by cards in three ways: by **title,** by **author,** and by **subject.** Since you already have the author and title on your bib. cards, look for the book in the "Author/Title" section of the card catalogue, a section well marked by "Author/Title" signs. (The other section of the card catalogue is marked "Subject".) Find the drawer with the beginning letters of the author's last name. Find the last name that you want alphabetically. If there are other authors by the same last name, as there usually are, go through the cards alphabetically by first names until you find your author. If you discover your author has written several books, because there are several cards with the author's name, use the title to find the proper card for your source. A unique call number is assigned to each book in the collection. Books on similar topics have similar call numbers, but your book has its own special number which makes it possible to locate the book on the shelves in the stacks. Copy the book's **call number** on your bib. card.

Figure 6.1 on page 140 shows two cards from the card catalogue, both from the "Author/Title" section. The first is an "author" card, the card you would find if you looked up the book by the author's name. The second is a "title" card, the one that you would find if you looked the book up by title.

The "Subject" section of the card catalogue is helpful if you know the subject that you are interested in but do not have a specific author or title. The subject headings are rather general, so you might find several books related in different ways to your topic. Look through the catalogue cards and make bib. cards for the most interesting ones. Remember to put down the call numbers. The subject section of the card catalogue is sometimes useful, but it is not complete. Your topic may not be included, or it may be included in such a general way that the book titles you find there do not really seem to relate to your topic. Don't worry — there are better ways of locating good books on your topic.

Figure 6.2 on page 141 shows two cards from the "Subject" catalogue. The same book appears under two subject categories in the card catalogue: "Technology — History" and "Imperialism — History." If you thought of looking for books under either of these two subject headings, you would have discovered this book.

If your research at home turned up the author and title of an article in a journal, you need to find the title of the journal in the "Subject/Title" section of the card catalogue. The card will tell you

```
303.483
H344t     Headrick, Daniel R.
            The tools of empire : technology and
          European imperialism in the nineteenth
          century / Daniel R. Headrick. -- New
          York : Oxford University Press, 1981.
            x, 221 p. ; 22 cm.
            Includes bibliographical references
          and index.


            1. Technology--History.
          2. Imperialism--History.  I. Title


VtU     07 JUL 81     6447296     VTUUat     80-18099
```

```
                      The tools of empire
303.483
H344t     Headrick, Daniel R.
            The tools of empire : technology and
          European imperialism in the nineteenth
          century / Daniel R. Headrick. -- New
          York : Oxford University Press, 1981.
            x, 221 p. ; 22 cm.
            Includes bibliographical references
          and index.

            1. Technology--History.
          2. Imperialism--History.  I. Title


VtU                                 VTUUat     80-18099
```

Figure 6.1 *Sample cards from "Author/Title" section of the card catalogue. Above, "author" card; below, "title" card.*

```
                    TECHNOLOGY--HISTORY.
303.483
H344t     Headrick, Daniel R.
            The tools of empire : technology and
          European imperialism in the nineteenth
          century / Daniel R. Headrick. -- New
          York : Oxford University Press, 1981.
            x, 221 p. ; 22 cm.
            Includes bibliographical references
          and index.

            1. Technology--History.
          2. Imperialism--History.  I. Title


VtU                                VTUUsc     80-18099
```

```
                    IMPERIALISM--HISTORY.
303.483
H344t     Headrick, Daniel R.
            The tools of empire : technology and
          European imperialism in the nineteenth
          century / Daniel R. Headrick. -- New
          York : Oxford University Press, 1981.
            x, 221 p. ; 22 cm.
            Includes bibliographical references
          and index.

            1. Technology--History.
          2. Imperialism--History.  I. Title


VtU                                VTUUsc     80-18099
```

Figure 6.2 *Two cards from "Subject" catalogue.*

the dates and volumes of the journal the library holds in its collection. Libraries try to develop a continuous sequence of each journal from the first issue to the present — what they call a "complete run" of that periodical. But many times the library will hold only an "incomplete run," having started to collect issues of the periodical sometime after its beginning, or having interrupted its subscription for some reason. Check the volume which contains the article and the date on your bib. card. If the library has your volume, copy out the call number for the periodical. (If your library does not have run of the journal that includes your volume, you may consider ordering that article through interlibrary loan. But for the moment, concentrate upon those sources which are readily available to you.)

Two cards for a journal appear in Figure 6.3. The journal is found by the first card, the "Title" card. It tells you that the library has the journal, but you need to flip this card to the second card to find whether the library has a "complete run" or not. This "Title" card also tells you that this particular journal has its own index, in two volumes, compiled at different times. The second card tells you that the library has a complete run of the journal, and the index as well.

In some libraries, journals may not appear in the card catalogue. They will be listed separately on an available list of journal holdings, either at the reference desk or at the circulation desk.

Now that you have found the call numbers to the sources you located from the reading list, you can go to the library stacks to find your material. If you have a campus library with closed stacks, fill out a call slip at the circulation desk and have someone get your sources for you. Call numbers have a broader meaning, in addition to allowing you to find materials in your local library.

CATALOGING SYSTEMS

The call numbers look as strange as they do because they follow a plan for grouping books into recognizable categories. There are two major cataloging systems: Library of Congress and Dewey Decimal. Your library uses one of these systems. It is important to have a general idea of how each system works, because they arrange

```
Per.  Journal of the history of ideas ...   v. 1-
        Jan. 1940-
        Lancaster, Pa., and New York, Journal of the
        history of ideas, inc., College of the city of
        New York, 1940-
          v. 26-1/2 cm. quarterly.
        Index:
          v.1-25, 1940-64. lv.
          v.26-30, 1065-69. 1 v.

      1. Philosophy-Period.  I. New York. City college.

B1.J75                     105                        42-51802

Library of Congress    [53g1/2]
```

```
Per.  Journal of the history of ideas.

      v.1-    1940-date


      Index:
        v.1-30 1940-69
```

Figure 6.3 *Sample "Journal" cards. Above, journal is located by title; below, the second card (directly behind title card) shows holdings. In this case, the library has a complete run of the journal, and the journal has an index.*

books in groups, and knowledge of these groups can often help you in your research.

The Library of Congress system uses the alphabet for the major divisions of books: history under "D," for instance; geography under "G"; political science under "J." The Library of Congress major classification letters are listed below:

Library of Congress Classification Schedules

A	General Works
B-BJ	Philosophy. Psychology
BL-BX	Religion
C	Auxiliary Sciences of History
D	History: General and Old World (Eastern Hemisphere)
E-F	History: America (Western Hemisphere)
G	Geography. Maps. Anthropology. Recreation
H	Social Sciences
J	Political Science
K	Law (General)
KD	Law of the United Kingdom and Ireland
KE	Law of Canada
KF	Law of the United States
L	Education
M	Music
N	Fine Arts
P-PA	General Philology and Linguistics. Classical Languages and Literatures
PA Supplement	Byzantine and Modern Greek Literature. Medieval and Modern Latin Literature
PB-PH	Modern European Languages
PG	Russian Literature
PJ-PM	Languages and Literatures of Asia, Africa, Oceania. American Indian Languages. Artificial Languages
P-PM Supplement	Index to Languages and Dialects
PN, PR, PS, PZ	General Literature. English and American Literature. Fiction in English. Juvenile Belles Lettres

PQ Part 1	French Literature
PQ Part 2	Italian, Spanish, and Portuguese Literatures
PT Part 1	German Literature
PT Part 2	Dutch and Scandinavian Literatures
Q	Science
R	Medicine
S	Agriculture
T	Technology
U	Military Science
V	Naval Science
Z	Bibliography. Library Science

In addition to the major classification by letter, additional letters and numbers follow to provide finer classification. In fact, the complete details of the Library of Congress classification system are published in 33 volumes! There are 218 captions for subclasses after the major classes, for example. A page from the *Outline* of the Library of Congress system related to history shows you the subdivisions:

History: General and Old World

Including geography and description of individual regions and countries

D		History (General)
	51-95	Ancient history
	111-203	Medieval history
	204-849	Modern history
	501-680	World War I
	731-838	World War II
	901-1075	Europe (General)
DA		Great Britain
	20-690	England
	700-745	Wales
	750-890	Scotland
	900-995	Ireland
DB		Austria. Czechoslovakia. Hungary
DC		France

DD		Germany
DE		The Mediterranean region. Greco-Roman world
DF		Greece
DG		Italy
DH-DJ		Netherlands. Belgium. Luxemburg
DJK		Eastern Europe
DK		Russia. Poland. Finland
DL		Northern Europe. Scandinavia
DP		Spain. Portugal
DQ		Switzerland
DR		Eastern Europe. Balkan Peninsula. Turkey
DS		Asia
DT		Africa
DU		Oceania (South Seas)
	80-398	Australia
	400-430	New Zealand
DX		Gypsies

The Dewey decimal system identifies the main divisions by numbers. History is listed under 900, for example. Social sciences appear under 300. The following is a list of the major categories of the Dewey Decimal Classification System. Notice how numbers serve for this system, instead of letters as in the Library of Congress system:

Dewey Decimal Classification System

000 GENERALITIES
010 Bibliographies & Catalogs
016 Bibliographies, Specific subjects
020 Library & information
030 General encyclopedic works
050 General serial publications
060 General organizations
070 Journalism, publishing, newspapers
080 General collections
090 Manuscripts & book rarities

100 PHILOSOPHY & RELATED DISCIPLINES
110 Metaphysics
120 Knowledge, cause, purpose, man
130 Popular & parapsychology, occultism
140 Specific philosophical viewpoints
150 Psychology
160 Logic
170 Ethics (Moral Philosophy)
180 Ancient, medieval, Oriental
190 Modern Western philosophy

200 RELIGION
210 Natural religion
220 Bible
230 Christian doctrinal theology
240 Christian moral & devotional
250 Local church & religious orders
260 Social & ecclesiastical theology
270 History & geography of church
280 Christian denominations & sects
290 Other religions & comparative

300 THE SOCIAL SCIENCES
310 Statistics
320 Political science
330 Economics
340 Law
350 Public administration
360 Social pathology & services
370 Education
380 Commerce
390 Customs & folklore

400 LANGUAGE
410 Linguistics
420 English & Anglo-Saxon languages
430 Germanic languages, German
440 Romance languages, French
450 Italian, Romanian, Rhaeto-Romanic

460 Spanish & Portuguese languages
470 Italic languages, Latin
480 Hellenic, Classical Greek
490 Other languages

500 PURE SCIENCES
510 Mathematics
520 Astronomy & allied sciences
530 Physics
540 Chemistry & allied sciences
550 Sciences of earth & other worlds
560 Paleontology
570 Life sciences
580 Botanical sciences
581 Zoological sciences

600 TECHNOLOGY (APPLIED SCIENCES)
610 Medical sciences
620 Engineering & allied operations
630 Agriculture & related
640 Domestic arts & sciences
650 Managerial services
660 Chemical & related technologies
670 Manufactures
680 Miscellaneous manufactures
690 Buildings

700 THE ARTS
710 Civic & landscape art
720 Architecture
730 Plastic arts, Sculpture
740 Drawing, decorative & minor arts
750 Painting & paintings
760 Graphic arts, Prints
770 Photography & photographs
780 Music
790 Recreational & performing arts

800 LITERATURE (BELLES-LETTRES)
810 American literature in English

820 English & Anglo-Saxon literatures
830 Literatures of Germanic languages
840 Literatures of Romance languages
850 Italian, Romanian, Rhaeto-Romanic
860 Spanish & Portuguese literatures
870 Italic languages literatures, Latin
880 Hellenic languages literatures
890 Literatures of other languages

900 GENERAL GEOGRAPHY & HISTORY
910 General geography, Travel
920 General biography & genealogy
930 General history of ancient world
940 General history of Europe
950 General history of Asia
960 General history of Africa
970 General history of North America
980 General history of South America
990 General history of other areas

Here is an example of the Dewey Classification for part of "General History of Europe":

940 General history of Europe Western Europe

.01–.09 Standard subdivisions, groups, regions, persons
As enumerated under 930–990

SUMMARY

940.1 Early history to 1453
.2 Modern period, 1453–
.3 World War I, 1914–1918
.4 Military history of World War I (Conduct of the war)
.5 20th century, 1918–

.1 Early history to 1453
Class here Middle Ages, 476–1453

[.*11*] Ancient history to ca. 499
(Use of this number is optional; prefer 936)

Class invasions and rise of new nations, ca. 500–799 [*formerly* 940.11] in 940.12

.12 Invasions and rise of new nations, ca. 500–799 [*formerly* 940.11]

We can understand the Dewey Classification call numbers for Daniel R. Headrick's *The Tools of Empire* (303.483), a book we used in Chapter 5, by looking at the numbers and topics below:

300 Social sciences

The sciences that deal with social activities and institutions

Class here behavioral sciences

Use 300.1–300.9 for standard subdivisions

Class a specific behavioral science with the subject, e.g., psychology 150; military, diplomatic, political, economic, social, welfare aspects of a war with history of the war

---

303 Social processes
For social interaction, see 302; relation of natural and quasi-natural factors to social processes, 304

.48 Causes of change
.482 Cultural exchange
Including social effects of international assistance
.483 Development of science and technology
.484 Purposefully induced change
Including social innovation, reform, dissent
Class social welfare services in 361–362
.485 Natural and social disasters
Examples: pandemics, wars

These classification systems are intended primarily for books, but they do include journals, as the example on page 143 shows. All periodicals appear in the card catalogue under their titles.

PERIODICALS

Periodicals publish on a regular, recurring basis. Often periodicals are more technically called "serials." Daily newspapers are periodicals as are weekly magazines, monthly magazines, quarterly research journals, annual summaries, and yearbooks. Recently, periodicals may take the form of regular issues of material on microfim or microfiche. Most libraries store their periodicals in three places: the current issues in the reading room, bound volumes of back issues in the stacks, and back issues on microfilm. Usually you must use periodicals in the library, although some libraries allow you to check out bound volumes for short periods. The microfilms need special viewers located in the microfilm room.

Journals are especially important for historical research because the editors of the various journals select articles of high quality in specified areas of history. Each journal tries to carve out a unique niche for itself, attracting specialized articles for a rather specialized readership. Journal articles are usually more helpful as sources of information for a short paper than are whole books on your topic, because the focus of the journal article is more specific and up to date.

Hundreds of historical periodicals are published in English, thousands worldwide. The following are some frequently used, readily available historical journals:

American Historical Review
Canadian Historical Review
English Historical Review
History
Isis, Journal of the History of Science
Journal of American History
Journal of Medieval and Renaissance Studies
Journal of Modern History
Journal of the History of Ideas
Renaissance Quarterly

Speculum

The Historian

More popular magazines and periodicals often contain very interesting articles to historians. The following is a list of useful and interesting popular periodicals:

American Heritage

Current History

Harper's

History Today

National Geographic

Newsweek

Scientific American

Smithsonian Magazine

Time

Yankee Magazine

The card catalogue and cataloging systems make it possible to store and retrieve both books and bound periodicals in your library. They also make your library research possible.

TWO RESEARCH STRATEGIES

Here's an entry in a student research log describing how one student got herself into research:

```
Getting started was definitely the most difficult
part of this research paper. Finding a topic that
is interesting and manageable is difficult when you
can write on just about anything. Once I found a
topic however and began to look up books and arti-
cles things began to progress naturally.
```

The "Self-Propelled" Mode of Research

It's good when research can begin "to progress naturally." But what to do if it doesn't go this smoothly? There are about as many ways to research as there are researchers. This guide has started you off on the research for your paper along what might be called the "internal" or "self-propelled" mode of research. You have decided upon your general topic as a result of thinking about your course and the required and recommended readings. You have some sources located from your required readings, from your textbook, or from suggestions by your professor or graduate assistant. These books and articles will have endnotes and bibliographies in them. If you build upon the material that you already have by mining that material for more bibliographic references, you may well be able to complete your research by yourself, without recourse to the reference section of your library. This is certainly NOT the most complete or thorough way of doing research, but it is very effective in getting you started. For now, let's try our first strategy.

You go to a specific section of the open stacks to locate your first book. The cataloging system that your library uses is about to work for you. Locate your book by using the call number. Take your book off the shelf, and STAY RIGHT THERE. Look at the books surrounding the book you have just found. There is a very good chance that there will be other books on the nearby shelves that will have sections or chapters related to your topic. Collect the most interesting ones from the shelves and look them over by checking their tables of contents and browsing through them. If they appear useful, make out bib. cards on the spot. Keep the ones that appear most useful and put the others on a library cart to be returned to the shelves by people who work in the library. (Most libraries do not want you to return books to the shelves yourself.) A misplaced book is a lost book.

You now have the original book and one or two others. Find your topic in these books by using the table of contents or the index at the back of the book. If the information they contain is useful, turn to their bibliographies and try to locate other books and especially articles in journals that seem appropriate. Check the endnotes to see if they mention other pertinent articles. Make a bib. card on anything that seems helpful; it's frustrating to lose good leads to sources.

By now you have additional bib. cards on your topic. Take

them to the card catalogue and look up the call numbers. Go to the stacks to find your books, and repeat this process. Searching the stacks in this way will turn up a wealth of information in books.

Next you should concentrate upon journal articles. If you have one from your original bib. cards with a call number, locate the bound volumes of that journal in the stacks and find the volume that contains your article. At a table close by, read the article quickly, paying special attention to the endnote references. If the article relates to your topic, there is a good chance the author will refer to other articles that will be useful to you as well. Make up bib. cards for each likely looking reference as soon as you find it. After reading your first article, look at your bib. cards. Check to see if any of the new references are to an article which was published in the same journal as your original article. If any were, go directly to the shelf and get the volume for your new article. Repeat the process with this new article, looking for additional sources, and making out bib. cards.

Most likely the new references will relate to articles published in different journals. Take your bib. cards to the card catalogue and look up the journals by title. Copy the call numbers, find the journals and the article that you are looking for, and repeat the research strategy above.

If you are alert in searching the references contained in the sources you find at first, you will be led to more than enough good material to complete your research assignment. This method works especially well for a short paper that only needs a limited number of substantial resources.

The steps in the "self-propelled" mode of research are easy to recap:

- Find references to sources in the materials that you have available to you at home, or from suggestions by your professor.
- Make bib. cards for these sources, look them up in the card catalogue, find them in the stacks, and mine them for new sources.
- Make bib. cards for the new sources that you have mined from the first sources, and use their endnotes and bibliographies for further sources.

- Stop when you have enough material to use to complete your assignment.

The "Reference" Mode of Research

The "reference" mode is the REAL way to do research. The "self-propelled" mode works best if you are already familiar and comfortable with the library and you do not need to exhaust the available resources for adequate treatment of your topic.

The "reference" mode will involve you with a great many aids to research, some rather complicated. Mastery of all the research aids available in the reference section will result in your finding EVERYTHING on your topic. The rest of this chapter is devoted to describing the resources available to students of history, at all levels, as they do their research. All of these resources are stored in the library's reference section.

HELP FROM THE REFERENCE SECTION

For your first encounter with the reference section, GET HELP! Using the reference section for the first time is like learning to sail a sailboard. You read the instruction book all winter, but now that you are standing in the water, it is nice to have a friend beside you who really knows what to do. If you have done some preparation and you have thought about your topic a bit, the reference librarian will be glad to help you. Bring a copy of the assignment sheet along to show to the librarian. You will be partners in your research effort. When you finish your research, and do well on your paper, remember to visit the reference librarian to show your paper. He or she will be as pleased as you are that your library research was successful!

Guides to Reference Books

The first places to start locating research materials are the guides to reference books contained in the reference section. These guides will give you brief descriptions of all of the various reference sources available in the reference section, such as abstracts and indexes. The following guides are especially helpful to historians:

Eugene P. Sheehy, *Guide to Reference Books,* 9th ed. Chicago: American Library Association, 1976. Supplement, 1980. Second Supplement, 1982. This is the standard guide to reference books. It replaces the earlier work by Constance Winchell.

Helen J. Poulton, *The Historian's Handbook, A Descriptive Guide to Reference Works.* Norman: University of Oklahoma Press, 1972.

Elizabeth Frick, *Library Research Guide to History,* "Library Research Guides" Series. No. 4. Ann Arbor, Michigan: Pierian Press, 1980. Appendix III "Basic Reference Sources for Courses in History."

Carla Stoffle and Simon Karter, *Materials and Methods for History Research,* New York: Neal-Schuman Publishers, 1979. "Instructor's Manual" and "Workbook."

Your reference librarian already knows about most of the resources described in these guides. That is only one of the reasons why reference librarians can be so helpful to you. At some point in your research career, especially if you plan to go on to graduate school, or to become a lawyer, or to work as a consultant, you will want to study these guides thoroughly by yourself. For now, begin your research by learning about Abstracts and Indexes.

Abstracts

Sheehy's *Guide to Reference Books* described many different abstracts. Abstracts give you information about articles by providing short descriptions, or abstracts, of what they contain. The card catalogue helped you with access to books. It also located the bound volumes of periodicals for you. But the card catalogue does not contain information about the articles which appear in the periodicals. You need to gain access to articles in different ways. Using the abstracts is one of the best ways. Two abstracts that are especially useful to historians are:

Historical Abstracts

Part A: Modern History Abstracts (1450–1914)
Part B: Twentieth Century Abstracts (1914–1980)

America: History and Life (Bibliographic entries on United States and Canadian history exclusively.)

Here are two descriptions of *Historical Abstracts* in Sheehy's *Guide to Reference Books,* the first from the 9th edition and the second from the Second Supplement, 1982:

Abstract journals

Historical abstracts, 1775–1945; bibliography of the world's periodical literature . . . Erich H. Boehm, ed. v.1, no.1–, March 1955–. Santa Barbara, Calif., Clio Pr. with the Internat. Social Science Inst., 1955–, v.1–. Quarterly. DA24

Publisher varies. Subtitle varies.

An abstract journal, with signed abstracts contributed by scholars, mainly from the United States. To 1964 covers the world's periodical literature on history from 1775 to 1945, in a classified arrangement with annual author, biographical, geographical, and subject indexes (these vary). After 1964 the United States and Canada are excluded (*see America: history and life,* DB29). Beginning v.17 (1971), published in two parts: A, Modern history abstracts, 1775–1914; B, Twentieth century abstracts. Now selectively indexes some 2,200 periodicals; includes abstracts of articles included in *Festschriften, Mélanges,* transactions and proceedings. D299.H5

——Five year index. v.1–5. 1963; v.6–10. 1965; v.11–15. 1970.

Includes subject and author indexes.

• • •

Abstract journals

Historical abstracts, v.26–. Santa Barbara, Calif., Amer. Bibliographic Center, 1980–. Service basis. 2DA3

For earlier volumes and annotation *see Guide* DA24.

v.26–30 (scheduled for publication 1980–85) will offer retrospective indexing of journals published 1954–79 which were not included in earlier volumes of this series. Extension of the period of coverage (now 1450 to the present) together with expanded coverage of journal titles necessitated the production of these additional volumes.

With v.31, 1980 (published concurrently with the retrospective volumes), coverage is further expanded to include citations for books and dissertations as well as abstracts for periodical articles. The dissertations are drawn from *Dissertation abstracts international* (and the listing is therefore not exhaustive); the books are selected from reviews in *Choice, Library journal* and 11 English-language history journals. v.31 will be issued in two fascicles for each part; with v.32 publication will resume the pattern of quarterly issues for each part.

The "List of periodicals surveyed for *America: history and life* and *Historical abstracts*," revised 1980, pp. 707–32 of v.26A gives the years of coverage for each indexed journal. D299.H5

——Five year index, v.16–20 (1970–74). 1979. 2v.

Let's use the *Historical Abstracts* for 1980 to look up Daniel R. Headrick, the author that we used in Chapter 5. We know from looking in his bibliography at the end of his book that he wrote an article on a topic similar to his book. This article was published in 1979, so we need to give the abstract service time to pick up the article. Here is what we find in the 1980 volume of the *Abstracts:*

31A:292. 19c
Headrick, Daniel R. THE TOOLS OF IMPERIALISM: TECHNOLOGY AND THE EXPANSION OF EUROPEAN COLONIAL EMPIRES IN THE NINETEENTH CENTURY. *J. of Modern Hist. 1979 51(2): 231–263.* Considers the technological advances that allowed or facilitated the European advance into Asia and Africa during the 19th century. The first of these was the river steamboat. The British used the *Diana* during the Burmese War of 1824–26. In 1832–34 Macgregor Laird, son of a shipbuilder, explored the Niger on two steamers. Other Laird-built iron steamers played a crucial role in the Opium War of 1840–42. After this, steamboats were an essential tool of European dominance in countries with navigable rivers. Until the mid-19th century, the European penetration of Africa was impeded by diseases which decimated exploratory and military missions. It was the prophylactic use of quinine against falciparum malaria, beginning in the 1850's, which opened the continent to large-scale European invasions. The power of European industrial technology was also directed at indigenous societies in the form of quick-firing rifles. The overwhelming superiority of European over non-Western weapons only came after the 1860's, however, with the

introduction of breechloaders, repeating rifles, and finally machine guns. These innovations led to one-sided massacres of attacking indigenous warriors by handfuls of European or European-led soldiers with modern weapons. Cheap victories in strategic offensives against Asians and Africans blinded European military thinkers to the defensive nature of the new rifles on the battlefield and led to overconfidence in World War I offensives. 112 notes. J/S

We can decide if the article is going to be useful for our research just by reading this abstract in the reference section of the library. We see that it is, so we fill out a bib. card, go to the card catalogue to find the call number for the *Journal of Modern History,* write the call number on our bib. card, and go to the stacks for the bound volume of the journal that contains the issue we need (Vol. 51, No. 2). The abstract gave us all the information that we needed to find the article.

Citation Indexes

Citation indexes are compiled to give the researcher information on where a work has been cited, or referred to. You can find where and how other historians have used the same work that you're using. The citation indexes can be used in conjunction with the abstracts, as you will see in our examples.

Two main sources of citations are useful to the historian:

Arts and Humanities Citation Index in three parts,
- Citation Index
- Source Index
- Permuterm Subject Index (set up for computer searching)

A multidisciplinary index of 6900 journals and selected books. 1300 journals are indexed fully, the rest selectively.

Social Sciences Citation Index, An International Multidisciplinary Index of the Literature of the Social, Behavioral, and Related Sciences
- Citation Index
- Source Index
- Permuterm Subject Index
- Journal Citation Reports

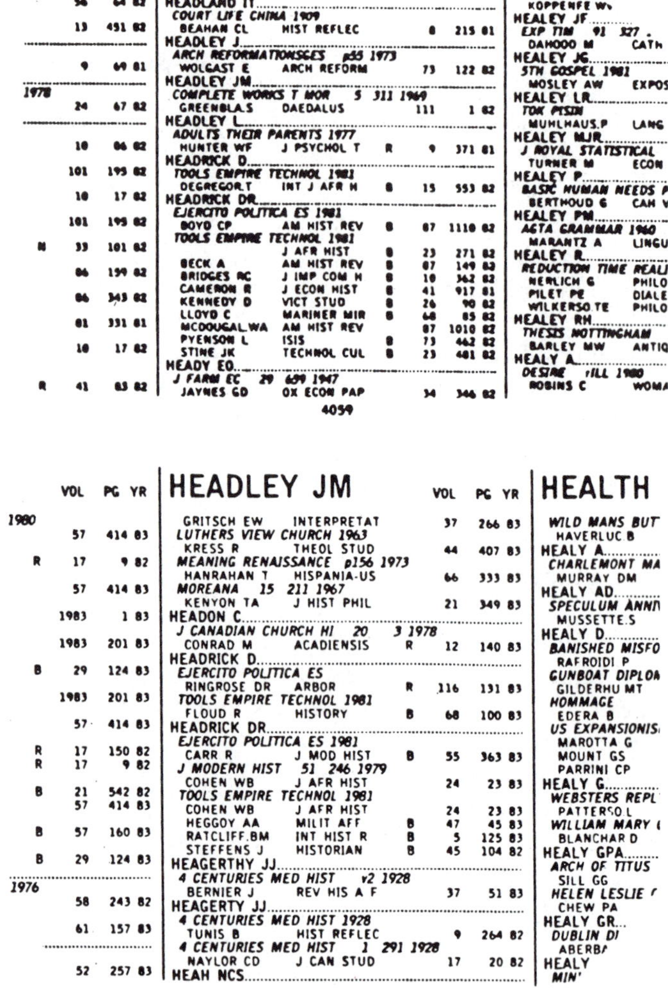

56 64 82
13 451 82
9 69 81
1978
24 67 82
10 86 82
101 195 82
10 17 82
101 195 82
N 33 101 82
86 159 82
86 343 82
81 331 81
10 17 82
R 41 83 82

HEADLAND IT
COURT LIFE CHINA 1909
BEAHAN CL HIST REFLEC 8 215 81
HEADLEY J
ARCH REFORMATIONSGES p55 1973
WOLGAST E ARCH REFORM 73 122 82
HEADLEY JM
COMPLETE WORKS T MOR 5 311 1969
GREENBLA S DAEDALUS 111 1 82
HEADLEY L
ADULTS THEIR PARENTS 1977
HUNTER WF J PSYCHOL T R 9 371 81
HEADRICK D
TOOLS EMPIRE TECHNOL 1981
DEGREGOR T INT J AFR H B 15 553 82
HEADRICK DR
EJERCITO POLITICA ES 1981
BOYD CP AM HIST REV B 87 1110 82
TOOLS EMPIRE TECHNOL 1981
J AFR HIST B 23 271 82
BECK A AM HIST REV B 87 149 82
BRIDGES RC J IMP COM H B 10 362 82
CAMERON R J ECON HIST B 41 917 81
KENNEDY D VICT STUD B 26 90 82
LLOYD C MARINER MIR B 68 85 82
MCDOUGAL WA AM HIST REV 87 1010 82
PYENSON L ISIS B 73 462 82
STINE JK TECHNOL CUL B 23 481 82
HEADY EO
J FARM EC 29 659 1947
JAYNES GD OX ECON PAP 34 346 82
4059

KOPPENFE W
HEALEY JF
EXP TIM 91 327
DAHOOD M CATH
HEALEY JG
5TH GOSPEL 1981
MOSLEY AW EXPOS
HEALEY LR
TOK PISIN
MUHLHAUS P LANG
HEALEY MJR
J ROYAL STATISTICAL
TURNER M ECON
HEALEY P
BASIC HUMAN NEEDS
BERTHOUD G CAH V
HEALEY PM
AGTA GRAMMAR 1960
MARANTZ A LINGU
HEALEY R
REDUCTION TIME REALI
NERLICH G PHILO
PILET PE DIALE
WILKERSO TE PHILO
HEALEY RH
THESIS NOTTINGHAM
BARLEY MW ANTIQ
HEALY A
DESIRE ILL 1980
ROBINS C WOMA

VOL PG YR
1980
57 414 83
R 17 9 82
57 414 83
1983 1 83
1983 201 83
B 29 124 83
1983 201 83
57 414 83
R 17 150 82
R 17 9 82
B 21 542 82
57 414 83
B 57 160 83
B 29 124 83
1976
58 243 82
61 157 83
52 257 83

HEADLEY JM VOL PG YR
GRITSCH EW INTERPRETAT 37 266 83
LUTHERS VIEW CHURCH 1963
KRESS R THEOL STUD 44 407 83
MEANING RENAISSANCE p156 1973
HANRAHAN T HISPANIA-US 66 333 83
MOREANA 15 211 1967
KENYON TA J HIST PHIL 21 349 83
HEADON C
J CANADIAN CHURCH HI 20 3 1978
CONRAD M ACADIENSIS R 12 140 83
HEADRICK D
EJERCITO POLITICA ES
RINGROSE DR ARBOR R 116 131 83
TOOLS EMPIRE TECHNOL 1981
FLOUD R HISTORY B 68 100 83
HEADRICK DR
EJERCITO POLITICA ES 1981
CARR R J MOD HIST B 55 363 83
J MODERN HIST 51 246 1979
COHEN WB J AFR HIST 24 23 83
TOOLS EMPIRE TECHNOL 1981
COHEN WB J AFR HIST 24 23 83
HEGGOY AA MILIT AFF B 47 45 83
RATCLIFF BM INT HIST R B 5 125 83
STEFFENS J HISTORIAN B 45 104 82
HEAGERTHY JJ
4 CENTURIES MED HIST v2 1928
BERNIER J REV HIS A F 37 51 83
HEAGERTY JJ
4 CENTURIES MED HIST 1928
TUNIS B HIST REFLEC 9 264 82
4 CENTURIES MED HIST 1 291 1928
NAYLOR CD J CAN STUD 17 20 82
HEAH NCS

HEALTH
WILD MANS BUT
HAVERLUC B
HEALY A
CHARLEMONT MA
MURRAY DM
HEALY AD
SPECULUM ANNI
MUSSETTE S
HEALY D
BANISHED MISFO
RAFROIDI P
GUNBOAT DIPLOM
GILDERHU MT
HOMMAGE
EDERA B
US EXPANSIONIS
MAROTTA G
MOUNT GS
PARRINI CP
HEALY G
WEBSTERS REPL
PATTERSO L
WILLIAM MARY
BLANCHAR D
HEALY GPA
ARCH OF TITUS
SILL GG
HELEN LESLIE
CHEW PA
HEALY GR
DUBLIN DI
ABERB
HEALY
MIN

Figure 6.4 *Entries for 1982 (above) and 1983 (below) from "Citation Index" of* Arts and Humanities Citation Index.

A multidisciplinary index of 4500 journals. 1400 are indexed fully, the rest selectively.

Let's look up Daniel R. Headrick's *The Tools of Empire* in the *Arts and Humanities Citation Index,* "Citation Index," for 1982 and 1983. We know that the book was published in 1981. Notice how inconsistent the journal editors were in handling the author's name. Because a few used only the first name, but not the middle initial, and the rest used both the author's first name and middle initial, there are two different entries for the same author.

The volumes of the "Citation Index" list the author that you are interested in, and they give different authors who have referred to your author in their journal articles. You see the author, the journals containing the article, the volume, page, and year in the citation. Notice that the last entry in the "Citation Index" for 1983 is:

STEFFENS, J HISTORIAN B 45 104 82.

This entry cites the book review we used as an example in Chapter 4.

If we turn to the "Source Index," we find more information on the source of the reference to Headrick's book. We find that the source of the citation is a book review, published in the journal *Historian,* and written by J. Steffens at the University of Vermont:

STEFFEN JO
COUES,ELLIOTT NATURALIST AND FRONTIER HISTORIAN - CUTRIGHT,PR, BROOHEAD,MJ ◆ BOOK REVIEW
N MEX HIST 58(2):190-191 83 1R
UNIV OKLAHOMA, NORMAN, OK 73019, USA
CUTRIGHT PR 81 E COUES NATURALIST F

STEFFEN W
THE SITUATION OF FREE LANCE COMPOSERS - (A FEW PRELIMINARY THOUGHTS)
INTERFACE 12(1-2):135-138 83 NO R
BERLINER HSCH MUS, BERLIN, FED REP GER

STEFFENS J
THE TOOLS OF EMPIRE - TECHNOLOGY AND EUROPEAN-IMPERIALISM IN THE 19TH-CENTURY - HEADRICK,DR ◆ BOOK REVIEW
HISTORIAN 45(1):104-105 82 1R
UNIV VERMONT, BURLINGTON, VT 05405, USA
HEADRICK DR 81 TOOLS EMPIRE TECHNOL

STEFFY JR
THE ATHLIT RAM, A PRELIMINARY INVESTIGATION OF ITS STRUCTURE
MARINER MIR 69(3):229-247 83 6R
INST NAUT ARCHAEOL, COLLEGE STN, TX 77840, USA
BASCH L 75 INT J NAUTICAL ARCHA 4 201
" 82 MARINERS MIRROR 68 3
CASSON L 71 SHIPS SEAMANSHIP ANC

Figure 6.5 *Entry from "Source Index" of the* Arts and Humanities Citation Index.

The *Arts and Humanities Citation Index* can also be used in conjunction with the various abstracts — *Historical Abstracts,* for example. Look up the authors who have referred to the book that you are using. The abstracts will tell you about their articles. If an article looks interesting, make out a bib. card, go to the card catalogue, and find the journal with the article. The citation index is therefore a good source of articles related to your topic. Usually authors who refer to the book you are using do so in articles on subjects related to your topic. The two examples that we have used give you 14 new possibilities for articles on your topic! Without the citation index, you would not have known about these articles. Now you can begin to track them down and select the most interesting ones in the reference section.

The other citation index historians use is the *Social Sciences Citation Index*. The reason that there are two is that sometimes history is considered one of the humanities and sometimes it is considered one of the social sciences. The two indexes use different lists of journals, but there is some overlap. Historians should check both citation indexes. Figure 6.6 shows entries from the "Citation Index" of the *Social Sciences Citation Index* for 1982 and 1983.

These citations turn up some of the same listings, as well as some new listings. Notice what has happened to poor Daniel R. Headrick in the two citation indexes: he has been listed as Headrick D, Headrick DK, and Headrick DR. We know they are the same Headrick, but the *American Historical Review* apparently got his middle initial wrong.

Between the two citation indexes, you have a wealth of possible new sources of information.

Other Helpful Indexes

Though there are many other indexes, here are three more especially useful to historians:

Humanities Index (Indexes primarily by subject of the article with a good book review section.)

Social Sciences Index (Indexes primarily by subject of the article with a good book review section.)

VOL PG YR
. 34 126
LEEP 5 5139 82
. 30 126
H NEVR PS 0 82 1015 82
ED DISO
DITIONAL CITATIONS
K# 24741 1982 5 82
SYCHOPHYSL 19 167 82
K# 24741 1982 411 82
PPL PSYCH 3 279 82
CLIN PSYC R 30 4 82
K# 26197 1982 453 82
K# 24930 6 59 81
K# 26001 1981 3 81
RES PERS 16 230 82
ED DISO 1
LIN PLAST 9 337 82
ED DISO 1 400
OGN SCI 6 1 82
AMA
K# 28431 2 203 81
ED DISO
DEV BEH P 3 127 82
K# 24741 1982 405 82
ED DISO 1 257
EV NEUROL 130 507 82
S 27 235
DITIONAL CITATION
NVIR RES 20 306 82
63 632
COT EDUC R 14 109 82
U 0485
K# 26600 1982 170 82
17 203
POL S 9 116 82
197
1 565 81
14 37 82
29 911 82
37 435 81

HEADLEY JC VOL PG YR
HEADLEY JC
67 PESTICIDE PROBLEM EC
RUTTAN VW SCIENCE 216 23 82
68 AM J AGR ECON 50
SUNDQUIS WB MINN AES SB 1982 R 1 82
72 PEST CONTROL STRATEG 100
SEE SCI FOR 1 ADDITIONAL CITATION
GETZ WM ANN R ENTOM R 27 447 82
TISDELL C J ENVIR SYS 12 153 82
HEADLEY JM
69 COMPLETE WORKS T MOR 5 311
GREENBLAS DAEDALUS 111 1 82
HEADLEY L
72 6TH P INT C SUIC PRE
75 SUICIDE DIFFERENT CU 215
BOLDT M OMEGA 13 145 82
77 ADULTS THEIR PARENTS
HUNTER WF J PSYCHOL T R 9 371 81
LIEBERMAS J FAM THER B 4 320 82
HEADRICK D
81 TOOLS EMPIRE TECHNOL
ROBERTS AF AM ETHNOL 9 712 82
HEADRICK DK
81 TOOLS EMPIRE TECHNOL
MCDOUGAL WA AM HIST REV 87 1010 82
HEADRICK DR
81 EJERCITO POLITICA ES
BOYD CP AM HIST REV B 87 1110 82
81 TOOLS EMPIRE TECHNOL
J AFR HIST B 23 271 82
BAGCHI AK ECON POLIT B 17 824 82
BECK A AM HIST REV B 87 149 82
CAMERON R J ECON HIST B 41 917 81
FAY PW J ASIAN ST B 41 807 82
PYENSON L ISIS B 73 462 82
STINE JK TECHNOL CUL B 23 401 82
VONTUNZE GM BUS HIST RE B 55 599 81
HEADRICK MR
76 FWSOBS76 US FISH W
SWALES S J ENVIR MGM 14 103 82
HEADRICK MW
69 J EXP PSYCHOL 79 486
ARABIAN JM PSYCHOPHYSL 19 206 82
SIMONS RF BIOL PSYCH 14 297 82
71 PSYCHOPHYSIOLOGY 8 132
JERN S ACT MED SC R 1982 1 82

HEAGERTY AM VOL PG YR
HEAGERTY AM
81 BRIT MED J 282 1971
LAMY PP J AM GER SO 30 5 11 82
HEAGERTY JJ
29 4 CENTURIES MED HIST
MARANO L CURR ANTHR 23 385 82
HEAKES FV
49 COMMUNICATION 1365
GREENHOU B J CAN STUD 16 133 81
HEAL
76 BU LR 56 449
CRASWELL R BOSTON U LR 62 661 82
HEAL DJ
78 NEUROPHARMACOLOGY 17 365
HEAL DJ NEUROPHARM 21 159 82
78 NEUROPHARMACOLOGY 17 1005
SEE SCI FOR 2 ADDITIONAL CITATIONS
ARATO M NEUROPSYCHB 8 162 82
NUTT DJ NEUROPHARM 21 601 82
80 NEUROPHARMACOLOGY 19 133
SEE SCI FOR 1 ADDITIONAL CITATION
COWEN PJ BR J PHARM 76 260 82
81 EUR J PHARMACOL 75 231
SEE SCI FOR 2 ADDITIONAL CITATIONS
BONDINEL WE ANNU REP M R 17 41 82
NUTT DJ NEUROPHARM 21 601 82
SUGRUE MF N-S ARCH PH 320 90 82
82 NEUROPHARMACOLOGY 21 159
NUTT DJ NEUROPHARM 21 601 82
HEAL F
80 PRELATES PRINCES STU
KITCHING C HISTORY B 66 507 81
LEHMBERG SE J MOD HIST B 54 179 82
YOUINGS J AM HIST REV B 86 1006 81
HEAL G
71 REV EC STUDIES
MAJUMDAR M J ECON THEO 27 101
73 THEORY EC PLANNING
ELSTER J BK# 27536 2 1
FUCHS G J ECON THEO R 26
75 THEORY EC PLANNING
ERICSON RE ECONOMETRIC 50
76 BELL J EC 7 371
FOURGEAU C J ECON DYN
KADEKODI G ECON POLIT 3
PIRDYCK RS J ENVIR EC
WITHAGEN C ECONOMIST

HEAD JG VOL PG YR
73 PUBLIC FINANCE PLANN 25
LEFF NH TRMES ECON 50 2193 83
74 PUBLIC GOOD PUBLIC W
SAREL D J MARKET E 47 103 83
PUBLIC GOODS PUBLIC
RAN C ENVIR PL A 15 1083 83
NAN G PUBL FIN Q 11 465 83
RTY TM CONFL MANAG 5 111 81
E W PHIL SOC CR 9 147 82
FINANCE FINAN 31 313
KYKLOS N 35 702 82
PUBL FINAN 37 387 82
227
FINAN 37 387 82
J 23 131 83
24 469 83
83
HEADRICK D
81 TOOLS EMPIRE TECHNOL
FLOUD R HISTORY B 46 100 83
6074

HEADRICK DR VOL PG YR
HEADRICK DR
79 J MODERN HIST 51 231
VAYRYNEN R INT SOC SCI 35 61 83
79 J MODERN HIST 51 246
COHEN WB J AFR HIST 24 23 83
81 EJERCITO POLITICA ES
LARR R J MOD HIST B 55 363 83
81 TOOLS EMPIRE
CHRISTOP AJ J HIST GEOG 9 309 83
81 TOOLS EMPIRE TECHNOL
BROOKFIE H INT SOC SCI 34 375 82
COHEN WB J AFR HIST 24 23 83
DUMOR EK SOC SCI J B 20 138 83
HEADRICK MW
69 J EXP PSYCHOL 79 486
ARABIAN JM PSYCHOPHYSL 20 325 83
NICHOLAS T PAV J BIOL 18 144 83
SIMONS RF BIOL PSYCH 17 193 83
SOMSEN RJM PSYCHOPHYSL 20 68 83
HEADRICK TE
73 CRISIS CHANGE HIST S
J ASIAN AFR 17 74 82
SERIES U 8 59
9 434 83

Figure 6.6 *Entries for 1982 (above) and 1983 (below) from "Citation Index" of* Social Sciences Citation Index.

British Humanities Index (Indexes about 300 journals, many British journals not picked up by the other indexes.)

Each of these indexes surveys different lists of journals.

Another important index is the *Essay and General Literature Index*. This is the source for "hidden articles," essays and articles which never will appear in the other indexes because they are included within collections of articles or essays. The collections will be indexed by editor and title, but the essays and articles within them will not. This index surveys thousands of articles and essays in hundreds of volumes each year, making them available to the researcher in the reference section.

The *Bibliographic Index, A Cumulative Bibliography of Bibliographies* 1937 to present, is very helpful. It's amazing how many bibliographies have been complied on how many different subjects over the years.

Periodicals

The standard guide to periodicals is *Ulrich's International Periodicals Directory*, 24th edition, 1985. The subtitle of this work is "A classified guide to current periodicals, foreign and domestic." This directory began in 1932 and now appears in two volumes. It shows you where the journal that you are interested in is indexed. Some journals provide their own cumulative index from time to time, the case with the *Journal for the History of Ideas* that we found in the card catalogue. But most do not. Knowing where the journal is indexed, such as the *Humanities Index*, saves you the trouble of going through the tables of contents of each bound volume of the journal, year after year.

Another very useful guide to periodicals is *Indexed Periodicals*, by Joseph V. Marconi. As the subtitle explains, the work is "A guide to 170 years of coverage in 33 indexing services."

The most widely known guide to periodicals is *Readers' Guide to Periodical Literature*. This is sometimes useful but it must be used with the knowledge of what it is actually doing for you. This guide definitely does not survey all popular periodicals. It does include about 150 periodicals, but they are a very mixed assortment.

Be sure to check the beginning of the guide for the list of periodicals that are surveyed. Historians should check this guide for the more popular articles on historical topics, but you need to go beyond the *Readers' Guide* to do historical research.

Newspaper Indexes

Newspapers are often an excellent source of information in addition to books and journal articles. Major newspapers are indexed. The two that you will most likely use in your research are:

New York Times Index, 1913–

Times Index, 1906– (London Times)

The Library of Congress publishes two reference works which are helpful in informing you whether newspapers are available for your research:

Newspapers on Microfilm: Foreign Countries, 1848–1972

Newspapers on Microfilm: United States, 1948–1972

Book Review Indexes

It is often very helpful to know what other historians have thought about a book that you are relying upon for your research. There are several convenient reference sources for book reviews:

Book Review Index. The BRI is a master key to book reviews in more than 455 publications. "It covers the major general interest literary and educational publications in fields of social sciences, humanities, natural sciences, and fine arts."

Current Book Review Citations. Covers 1000 periodicals, fiction, non-fiction, foreign language, and new editions included.

Book Review Digest, 1905–. A book must have received three or more reviews to be included in this digest. The BRD covers books in the humanities, social sciences, and general science. It has relatively limited coverage of historical journals.

Two sources of information for reviews of history books are:

History: Reviews of New Books

Reviews in American History

Atlases and Chronologies

Historians need to be oriented in both space and time. The reference section has atlases and chronologies that will give you an overview of your topic. The following are very helpful:

Grun, Bernard. *The Timetables of History: A Horizontal Linkage of People and Events.* New York: Simon and Schuster, 1975.

Langer, William L. *An Encyclopedia of World History: Ancient, Medieval and Modern Chronologically Arranged.* 5th ed. Boston: Houghton Mifflin, 1972.

Palmer, Robert R. *Atlas of World History.* Chicago: Rand, McNally, 1957.

Sheperd, William R. *Sheperd's Historical Atlas.* 9th ed. New York: Barnes and Noble, 1973.

Interlibrary Loan

If you are researching in the "reference mode," using the resources in the reference section of the library, you will often turn up references to books and articles that your library does not have in its holdings. Continue your search for materials, and get a good idea of just what your library does have related to your topic. It will be rare that your own library does not have enough information for you to use for short paper assignments. But if you are undertaking a major research paper, for a senior research project, for example, and you discover that almost all the references to your topic are in publications your library does not possess, **you need to change your topic.** You can complete a successful research project only when resources are available in your own library. Professional historians and some graduate students solve this resource problem by traveling to major research libraries for extended stays — not realistic for most undergraduates. It is **much** easier to change your topic when you discover resource materials are not readily available than it is to fight an uphill battle to collect information.

Although you cannot rely upon interlibrary loan for the major portion of your research material, your library can obtain research materials in limited quantities from any other library. Be sure that you look up the book or article that you think you need in the indexes and abstracts so you are sure it is really something that you need. Armed with information about your material, and convinced that you really need the resource, see your reference librarian to help you order the material through interlibrary loan. Usually the process takes several weeks. If you are requesting an article from a journal, expect to pay for Xeroxing fees. Clearly interlibrary loan should be your last resort.

THE RESEARCH LOG

Here are students' insights about doing research and writing as they reflect on their experiences in their research log:

> After reading and reading and taking note cards I began to write at the point when I felt I had learned enough about the topic to sit down and start writing without having to continually look up things. There was a point in my research when things began to seem repetitious, or merely someone's personal interpretation. At the point that I could see this I knew that I could begin writing originally. The first draft mainly involved compiling information into an order appropriate for a paper. After creating a rough outline and dividing my note cards into categories I could begin to see an essential order emerge from all of my research. Actually writing things down and seeing the concrete manifestation of this abstract concept of the "paper" brought out a lot of new ideas and connections and also helped me to see what I needed more facts about and what I needed to cut out entirely.
>
> My frustrations came with the final draft. I realized I had too much information. I hesitated to leave many things out because I felt I was not giving full scope to my topic – not exactly "telling

> it like it was" (in my mind, anyway). I actually found, though, that the paper became a more self-contained and focused unit through my having to limit my topic to 25 pages. I still want to write a longer more in-depth paper on the topic but I think that my final project maintained an edge through having to be concise and to the point.

. . .

> What seems to work is to find 2 or three relevant sources and then work from source to other sources. This same technique of moving from a good source found through the reference section to other good sources seems the most effective method of gathering books as well. Though in the case of books there is definite benefit in simply browsing the stacks in the area where a resource has been found or even where you looked at a book which was not useful.

Part of the reason for doing a research paper is to learn about the topic of the paper. The other part, perhaps equal to the first, is to learn how to be a historian by writing history. History is an active discipline. In order to be a historian, you need to do research, and you need to write history. More than that, you need to think about what you are doing. Too often, the pressure of doing the research and meeting the paper deadline makes it difficult to reflect upon what really happens. This is why keeping a research log is so valuable.

Keeping a research log as you go along in the process of doing your research and writing enables you to produce a record that you can reflect upon after the paper is completed. Your research log will be a running record of what you observe yourself doing as you work as a historian. Your own log entries will make it possible for you to be aware of what happens when you go about writing history.

Your research log should be informal, perhaps part of your class journal. (See suggestions in Chapter 2.) You should make regular short entries as you go along, each with a date. Make entries on things like the following:

- Getting started
- What did I know about my topic before I started?
- Finding a topic.
- Finding a focus.
- Where did I begin my research?
- How did I decide what material to include and what material to leave out?
- When did I begin to write?
- What was the interaction between writing and reading the research materials?
- How did I produce my first draft?
- What was most helpful in the process of revision of the draft?
- Did I feel like a historian as I did my research and writing?

After keeping your research log, and after finishing your paper, sit down with your log and read the entries over to yourself. What do you see yourself doing as you did your research and writing? Write a synopsis of your activities in writing history as a long entry in your journal. Think about questions like these as you write your synopsis:

1. How did I go about getting started on my research paper?
2. How did the reading of the research material and the writing of parts of the drafts of the paper affect one another?
3. How did I go about producing my first complete draft?
4. What was most helpful in the process of revision to produce the final paper?

Doing research in the library, writing history, and thinking about what you are doing by writing a synopsis of your research log will combine to make you a better historian.

Computer Searching

Computers and microcomputers are at the heart of a quiet revolution going on in libraries today. Your library may already have a computerized card catalogue and computer facilities for doing bibliographic searches. You may be able to take advantage of the computer's powerful information-processing capabilities to help you with your research. Computers in your library will help you search through the library's holdings and conduct general bibliographic searches. Most libraries are beginning to convert their card catalogues to on-line computer catalogues or they have already converted them. This means that all of the information on the cards in the card catalogue has been put into a computer. Computerized card catalogues make finding call numbers much faster and easier. If your library has an on-line catalogue, use it in the same way that you would the card catalogue with real, but "old fashioned" cards, described earlier in this chapter. Follow the instructions that your library provides for its particular computer system.

The bibliographic searches described in previous sections of this chapter can be more rapid and effective using a computer. Many of the abstracts and indexes discussed earlier, including *Historical Abstracts* and *Social Sciences Citation Index,* are available to libraries in both published and computerized forms. The computer versions of these abstracts and indexes are usually available through a computer search service in the reference section, or in an information retrieval lab.

The computer forms of abstracts, indexes, and other bibliographic tools are called *bibliographic databases.* They contain brief citations or descriptions of books, journal articles, conference reports, dissertations, and similar materials. The process of scanning or looking at these citations is called *computer searching* or *on-line searching.* In this process the searcher uses a computer to reach the database and to select certain citations by familiar *access points.* Access points to the bibliographic database can be author's names, titles of books or articles, or subject headings. The end product of the search is a printout of a customized bibliography of citations on a particular topic or by a certain author.

There are several advantages to computer searching compared to using print sources and making out bib. cards. The search process is very fast using a computer. Search times can average five to fifteen minutes, depending on the complexity of the questions. Bibliographic databases are not divided into yearly volumes like print versions, so you can search a subject through all available years at one time. In most print resources, you can look only under author's names, subject headings, or keywords from titles to find information. Using a computer you can also search for combinations of keywords. You can also often specify the language, publication type (such as book review or journal article), and years of publication. These added refinements can produce a bibliography tailor-made to your research topic.

Computer searching has some important disadvantages. These disadvantages are more evident in history than they are in other disciplines. Bibliographic databases were originally developed as part of the process of computerized typesetting. This means that indexing coverage began in the late 1960's and early 1970's. Disciplines such as medicine and the sciences depend upon the most recent information. Ten-year-old information is "old information" for these fields. The databases in medicine and the sciences are continually updated. Computer searching provides the doctor or scientist with citations of the most recent and therefore usually the most useful information. There are many more databases in medicine, science, and business now than in the humanities.

In contrast, historians need new information, old information, and all kinds of information in-between. Computer searching provides only a small portion of the coverage of material that historians require. Bibliographic databases are improving rapidly, but the historian must still use the reference section of the library to supplement the computer search.

Another difficulty associated with computer searching is learning the necessary "language" to conduct the search. The searcher has to learn the technical commands that form the language of the system used to communicate with the computer. There is no single standard set of commands for all systems. It is not yet possible to use plain English to communicate with the computer about your bibliographic search.

Computer searching also costs money. Searchers are charged for the time spent using the database, plus royalties for each citation selected. You also need to pay for long-distance telephone time if the database system requires communication with a central computer. To eliminate the need to contact a distant central information storage facility over long-distance telephone lines, your library might pay an expensive subscription fee to use a compact disc version of the same database right in your library. Depending upon the database system used and upon the complexity of the research question, computer searches may cost a few dollars to a few hundred dollars for each search.

Databases of particular interest to historians include:

Historical Abstracts

America: History and Life

Arts and Humanities Search

Social Scisearch

Dissertation Abstracts Online

Humanities Index

Social Science Index

Historical Abstracts and *America: History and Life* are produced by ABC–Clio Information Services. They correspond to the printed sources of the same name, but coverage for the computer version of *Historical Abstracts* dates from 1973, for *America: History and Life* from 1964. Like the printed versions, they index journal articles and selected books in history and include descriptive abstracts.

Arts and Humanities Search and *Social Scisearch* from the Institute for Scientific Information correspond to the printed versions, *Arts and Humanities Citation Index* and *Social Sciences Citation Index*. Computerized coverage extends from 1980 and 1972 respectively.

Dissertation Abstracts Online, a guide to American doctoral dissertations, corresponds to *Dissertation Abstracts International* in print. It is one of the few databases with a long time span. Coverage begins with 1861. All subject areas are included.

Humanities Index and *Social Sciences Index* are very new databases. They are produced by the H. W. Wilson Company, who also publish the print version. Their coverage begins in 1984.

Let's do a comparison between the search in the printed sources that we conducted earlier in this chapter and a computer search. Here is a simple search on *Historical Abstracts* on the author Daniel Headrick and the subject "imperialism." The search is described step-by-step, as the computer is used for the search. Refer to Figure 6.7 for each step.

Figure 6.7 Historical Abstracts *computer search.*

```
File 39:HISTORICAL ABSTRACTS - 73-86/ISS37B2
(Copr. ABC Clio Inc.)

      Set  Items  Description
      ---  -----  -----------

? s au=headrick, daniel?

      S1          6  AU=HEADRICK, DANIEL?
? s s1 and imperialism

                6  S1
             2798  IMPERIALISM
      S2        2  S1 AND IMPERIALISM
? t 2/5/1-2

2/5/1

1034970    33A-07098
  The Tools of Empire: Technology and European Imperialism
in the Nineteenth Century.
  Headrick, Daniel R
  Source: New York: Oxford U. Pr., 1981. 221 pp.
  Document Type: BOOK
  Descriptors: 19c ; Technology ; Europe ; Imperialism
  Historical Period: 1800H

2/5/2

996252    31A-00292
  THE TOOLS OF IMPERIALISM: TECHNOLOGY AND THE EXPANSION
OF EUROPEAN COLONIAL EMPIRES IN THE NINETEENTH CENTURY.
  Headrick, Daniel R
  J. of Modern Hist. 1979 51(2): 231-263.
  Note: 112 notes.
  Document Type: ARTICLE
  Considers the technological advances that allowed or fa-
cilitated the European advance into Asia and Africa during
the 19th century. The first of these was the river steam-
boat. The British used the Diana during the Burmese War of
1824-26. In 1832-34 Macgregor Laird, son of a shipbuilder,
explored the Niger on two steamers. Other Laird-built iron
steamers played a crucial role in the Opium War of 1840-
```

Figure 6.7 *Continued*

```
42. After this, steamboats were an essential tool of Euro-
pean dominance in countries with navigable rivers. Until
the mid-19th century, the European penetration of Africa
was impeded by diseases which decimated exploratory and
military missions. It was the prophylactic use of quinine
against falciparum malaria, beginning in the 1850's, which
opened the continent to large-scale European invasions.
The power of European industrial technology was also di-
rected at indigenous societies in the form of quick-firing
rifles. The overwhelming superiority of European over non-
Western weapons only came after the 1860's, however, with
the introduction of breechloaders, repeating rifles, and
finally machine guns. These innovations led to one-sided
massacres of attacking indigenous warriors by handfuls of
European or European-led soldiers with modern weapons.
Cheap victories in strategic offensives against Asians and
Africans blinded European military thinkers to the defen-
sive nature of the new rifles on the battlefield and led
to overconfidence in World War I offensives. (J/S)
  Descriptors: 19c ; Imperialism ; Technology ; Europe
  Historical Period: 1800H
? logoff

        16jun86 13:21:02 User02
  $1.49    0.023 Hrs File39
         $0.00  2 Types in Format  5
  $0.00  2 Types
  $0.25  Telenet
  $1.74  Estimated cost this file
  $2.06  Estimated total session cost  0.032 Hrs.
```

After you establish a connection with the database (File 39:HISTORICAL ABSTRACTS), the computer prompts you for an information request with a question mark (?). Using the language of the system, you type a set of commands that mean "select citations by the author Daniel Headrick" (s au=headrick, daniel ?). The computer responds that there are six citations by him in the database (S1 6 AU=HEADRICK, DANIEL ?). Because you are doing research on imperialism, you ask the computer to select only those citations by Headrick in which the word "imperialism" occurs (s s1 and imperialism). The system responds that there are two (S2 2 S1 AND IMPERIALISM). The computer prompts you with a question mark. You type a string of commands that tells the computer to print all of the information available on those two records (t 2/5/1–2), and then sign off. The computer prints out the information in Figure 6.7. Then it automatically tells you how much this search has cost. The computer search took 0.023 hours and cost $1.49 to obtain the information.

The citations illustrated by this search are in a standard format used in bibliographic databases. They do not look exactly like the citations in the printed reference sources, but they do contain the same elements of information. The text of the abstract is the same as that on pages 158–59.

Each campus library will have a different system for handling computer search requests. Some libraries will teach you how to search on the microcomputers provided for you to use. Other libraries will have you make an appointment with a librarian. The librarian will use the computer and you will get the search results. Payment requirements vary as well. Some libraries will pay for the search on their budget and not charge you at all. Some libraries will charge you the full amount of the cost for the search. There are all possible variations of payment requirements between these two.

The best way to find out about computer searching in your library is to go to the reference desk and ask the librarian. In years to come, computer searching will be a standard part of your library research.

FURTHER THOUGHTS ON WRITING HISTORY

Historians on Research

"The most important thing about research is to know when to stop."

"Research is endlessly seductive; writing is hard work."

Barbara Tuchman

"What I offer you here is in part my invention, but held tightly in check by the voices of the past."

Natalie Zemon Davis

"... no one can profit by historical research, or not much, unless he does some for himself."

Carl Becker

"... I have endeavored to let black women speak for themselves. I hope and trust the rich material here uncovered will stimulate new interpretations and, above all, further research into the black past."

Gerda Lerner

[7] Documentation Techniques

PREVIEW: *Accurate and proper documentation techniques help both the writer and the reader. Documentation usually means giving proper credit for borrowed information. But it also allows the reader to give full credit to the writer for the original or unique aspects of a piece of writing. Endnotes and bibliographic citations are not just mechanical nuisances. They provide important information.*

There is no standard documentation system accepted by all historians. Some historians consider history more of a social science and so prefer a form of documentation closer to that used in the sciences and social sciences. Other historians consider history to be one of the humanities, preferring a form of documentation similar but not identical to that used in literature and the arts. The Chicago Manual of Style *is widely accepted by historians. This is the general guide for the documentation in this book.*

Uses of bibliographic references
- *Comprehensive bibliographies*
- *Selected bibliographies*
  - *Guidelines to the evaluation of source materials*
  - *Annotated bibliographies*
  - *Bibliographical essays*
- *What do you need to cite in your endnotes?*
- *Endnote citation format*
- *Guides to style*
- *Additional examples of documentation*

Recently Daniel Beaupre, a student in a European Civilization course, came by with a fine paper on British Imperialism in India, "The Sepoy Rebellion." Proud of the paper, he wanted to thank his teacher for the use of an 1891 edition of the *Encyclopaedia Britannica*. In an earlier visit, he had looked up several articles related to his topic in that set. He said how delighted he had been to find an article by "a very knowledgeable writer" to supplement his information from other books and journal articles. The professor, glad that his set of encyclopedias had helped, asked "Who was the author?" Daniel turned to his bibliography to find out. His bibliographic citation for the article was incomplete, with neither the title of the article nor the author. He had noted the volume and the page of the article, but he had not read the Roman numerals for the volume accurately. Since the encyclopedias were in the office and they now both wanted to know the author of the article, he pulled the volume listed in his bibliography off the shelf. After a hurried search, he exclaimed, "Something is funny, the article isn't there any more!"

The end of the story is a happy one. The student found the article and its author, who turned out to be a Director General of Statistics to the Government of India, W.W. Huntley, "the very knowledgeable author." Daniel Beaupre was delighted to find that he had evaluated his source accurately. He had guessed that the author was knowledgeable from the internal evidence in the article, but knowing the proper bibliographic information confirmed his guess. Correcting his bibliographic citation made it certain that he would be able to find the article again.

USES OF BIBLIOGRAPHIC REFERENCES

After your research and writing are almost complete, preparing a bibliography often seems to be an unnecessary nuisance. But bibliographic references which include information about the author, title of the work, and date are important to both the writer and the reader. The writer needs to know the date the article or book was written because the date tells how close the author was in time to the event described. The date also tells the researcher whether the writer wrote before major recent studies in the subject, or before studies using new research techniques such as quantitative methods or demographics. The researcher also needs to know if the author is a recognized authority on the subject or may be known for work in a very different area. Barbara Tuchman's book, *A Distant Mirror, The Calamitous 14th Century,* is a famous example. Since she is well known as one of the best scholars on World War I and Europe before the Great War, Tuchman's venture into the 14th century raised interest and alerted readers that hers is likely to be a new kind of book about the Middle Ages.

The reader also needs accurate bibliographic citations, not because the professor insists upon it, but because the interested reader wants to make a judgment about the importance of the sources used in the writing of the history. Accurate citations also help the reader to go directly to the sources of information. Bibliographies provide one of the best places to start your own research project, as we saw in Chapter 6.

Bibliographies also tell the reader about the extensiveness of the research, the kinds of sources used, and the number of disciplines considered in the research. Were professional journal articles considered in the research in addition to books? Were the journals from a broad range of historical sub-disciplines, and from disciplines outside of history, such as philosophy, anthropology, geography, sociology, or political science? The bibliography provides a record of the writer's research. It allows the reader to follow the path of the writer's research and to make a judgment about the piece of history.

COMPREHENSIVE BIBLIOGRAPHIES

Bibliographies can be of several types. Some bibliographies attempt to include all relevant source material on the topic — from journals, books, manuscripts in archives, photographic collections, and map collections. This type of bibliography is very common in biographies, for example, because the author tries the make his work definitive, the most complete and comprehensive work possible. They are very helpful, allowing the researcher to start with all, or most, of the information about that special topic identified, at least to the point that the bibliography was prepared. (Books and articles take months, and usually years, to appear after the author completes the manuscript. The date that the author used to end his preface in a book, for example, is usually a year or two earlier than the date of publication. The date on the number and volume of the journal in which the article appears is usually a year or so later than the completion of the bibliography.) While these complete bibliographies are useful and save us time and work, they are usually not the kind of bibliographies that students are expected to prepare.

SELECTED BIBLIOGRAPHIES

Student bibliographies, for short papers and term papers, might best be called "selected bibliographies." These bibliographies contain all works the student actually consulted while preparing the paper, whether information from these works actually found its way specifically into the context of the paper and an endnote citation or not. These bibliographies, included at the end of a paper, give the reader a good sense of the kind and extent of information used in the preparation of the paper. Here's where bib. cards help you produce an accurate bibliography.

Guidelines to the Evaluation of Source Material

The best bibliographies for student papers are annotated bibliographies and bibliographic essays. These forms of bibliographies require that the writer evaluate the source of information and discriminate among the sources to identify the best and those of lesser value. The process of evaluating sources and discriminating among them requires careful thought and attention. Here are some guides to help you evaluate a book or an article for an annotated bibliography or bibliographic essay:

1. Begin by identifying the author's point of view. What is the frame of reference and how does he view his subject?
2. Identify the author's major historical hypotheses.
3. Identify the most important pieces of evidence that the author uses to support each historical hypothesis.
4. Think about the whole structure of the article or book. Have you identified the main historical hypotheses, along with the supporting evidence? Are there too many hypotheses? Are some of the hypotheses asserted rather than supported? Can you see

coherence both in the hypotheses and in the support for the hypotheses?

5. Think about the quality of the evidence offered in support of the author's hypotheses. Are you satisfied that the evidence was used well? Are the author's sources of information important and extensive? Be sure to investigate the author's bibliography and footnote citations carefully. They reveal the record of research.
6. Are you satisfied that the author's point of view towards the topic is appropriate? Has he or she chosen the more important, or the best hypotheses related to the topic? Do you fully understand the author's intentions in writing the work?

Annotated Bibliographies

Having considered each author's use of evidence and major hypotheses, you are in a position to evaluate and compare sources. Which do you have the most confidence in? Which are the best? Which are not as useful for the purposes of your paper topic?

You can convey the results of your own evaluation of sources to your reader in the form of an annotated bibliography. Let your reader know what you discovered about your sources. Your annotations may be brief like the following examples from a student paper on Kafka and Vienna:

Botstein, Leon. "The Viennese Connection." Partisan Review 49 (1982): 262-273. Explores the recent popularity of Viennese studies.

Brod, Max. Franz Kafka: A Biography. Trans. by G. Humphreys Roberts and Richard Winston. New York: Schocken Books, 1960. Brod stresses his friend Kafka's positive attitude towards life and the transcendental element in his writings.

Salten, Felix. "Aus den Anfangen: Erinnerungskizzen." Jahrbuch deutscher Bibliophilen und Literaturfreunde 18/19 (1932-1933): 31-46. Reminiscences of Cafe Griendsteidle by the creator of Bambi.

The major purpose of the annotated bibliography is to help the reader, but it also gives the writer practice in the discrimination of resource materials.

WRITING 7.1: ANNOTATED BIBLIOGRAPHY. Use the guidelines to the evaluation of source material to prepare an annotated bibliography for your research paper. Think about the sources that you are using for that paper and write short, helpful comments to your reader for each source that you list in your bibliography.

Bibliographical Essays

The bibliographical essay also provides annotations to the resource materials cited. The main difference between the bibliographical essay and the annotated bibliography is that the essay allows the author to take the citations out of sequencial alphabetical order and group the resources into interesting packets. The following is an excerpt from the bibliographical essay in Daniel R. Headrick's *The Tools of Empire:*

Bibliographical Essay

The information contained in this book came from hundreds of sources, most of them cited in the footnotes. Of the published sources, a few dozen were especially helpful, and I recommend them to the reader wishing to pursue certain topics in greater detail. For a general introduction to the theme, see Daniel R. Headrick, "The Tools of Imperialism: Technology and the Expansion of European Colonial Empires in the Nineteenth Century," *Journal of Modern History* 51, no. 2 (June 1979):231–63.

Part One: Steamboats and Quinine,
Tools of Penetration

For the early history of steamboats in Asia, see Henry T. Bernstein, *Steamboats on the Ganges: An Exploration in the History of India's Modernization through Science and Technology* (Bombay, 1960), a model monograph in the social history of technology; H. A. Gibson-Hill, "The Steamers Employed in Asian Waters, 1819–39," *The Journal of the Royal Asiatic Society, Malayan Branch* 27 pt. 1 (May 1954):127–61; and Gerald S. Graham, *Great Britain in the Indian Ocean: A Study of Maritime Enterprise, 1810–1850* (Oxford, 1968).

The most readable recent account of the Opium War is Peter Ward Fay, *The Opium War, 1840–1842: Barbarians in the Celestial Empire in the Early Part of the Nineteenth Century and the War by which They*

Forced Her Gates Ajar (Chapel Hill, N.C., 1975). On the steamers employed in that war, see William Dallas Bernard, *Narrative of the Voyages and Services of the Nemesis from 1840 to 1843,* 2 vols. (London, 1844), but note that there is a second edition of this work (London, 1845) and a third edition: Captain William H. Hall (R.N.) and William Dallas Bernard, *The Nemesis in China, Comprising a History of the Late War in that Country, with a Complete Account of the Colony of Hong Kong* (London, 1846). See also Gerald S. Graham, *The China Station: War and Diplomacy 1830–1860* (Oxford, 1978).

Steamers in the European penetration of Africa are best described in Macgregor Laird and R. A. K. Oldfield, *Narrative of an Expedition into the Interior of Africa, by the River Niger, in the Steam-Vessels Quorra and Alburkah, in 1832, 1833, and 1834,* 2 vols. (London, 1837); Christopher Lloyd, *The Search for the Niger* (London, 1973); and André Lederer, *Histoire de la navigation au Congo* (Tervuren, Belgium, 1965).

Still the best biography of Peacock is Carl Van Doren, *The Life of Thomas Love Peacock* (London and New York, 1911).

Malaria and quinine prophylaxis in the penetration of Africa are dealt with in Philip D. Curtin, *The Image of Africa: British Ideas and Actions 1780–1850* (Madison, Wis., 1964), a brilliant piece of historical research; but see also Michael Gelfand, *Rivers of Death in Africa* (London, 1964).

WHAT DO YOU NEED TO CITE IN YOUR ENDNOTES?

This question usually causes a lot of unnecessary worry and concern. The short answer is "everything that you take from some easily identifiable source that is not your own idea or information." But what does that mean?

Your note cards are full of all kinds of information, including the sources of that information. You copied out interesting quotations from books and articles. You extracted specific supporting information, or statistics for some argument or hypothesis. You noted some particular interpretation, or point of view, or hypothesis presented by one author. When the time comes to draft your paper, if you decide to use a quotation, or a set of statistics, or a special argument presented by one of your authors, you need to provide an endnote citation.

Endnotes help both readers and writers. They help readers to assess the quality of the information used directly in the paper. Endnotes also alert them to special points of view or arguments, and let them know where the supporting information comes from.

Endnotes also help the writers because they allow readers to distinguish the author's originality and the points of view. Since endnotes indicate material that authors have borrowed from some specifiable source, sections of the paper that do not have endnote citations represent the writer's own contribution to the topic. The reader knows where to give credit, where credit is due.

ENDNOTE CITATION FORMAT

Endnote citations relate directly to your bibliography because every source of information that you cite in your endnotes will appear in your bibliography. (You already know that because the headings of all of your note cards are keyed to your bib. cards, described in Chapter 5.) The converse is not true. All of the sources cited in your bibliography will not appear as cited works in your endnotes. The bibliography contains all of the works that you found and read in order to write your paper. The endnotes contain citations to the works from which you obtained specific information or data, specific arguments or ideas, or quotations.

The information in the endnote is similar to that in the bibliographical citation, but the form is not the same. The main difference is that the endnote uses the author's name in its natural order, first name first. The endnote also uses commas and parentheses as punctuation between the author's name, title of the work, and publication information, rather than periods. Endnotes are not indented and they usually contain page numbers. The page numbers are separated from a book citation by a comma and from a journal article citation by a colon. Endnote citations are numbered to correspond to the numbers placed in the text of your paper. Bibliographic citations are arranged in alphabetical order.

This sounds more complicated than it is; here are comparative examples:

Endnotes

1. Daniel R. Headrick, The Tools of Empire, (New York: Oxford University Press, 1981), 150–6.
2. Headrick, 180–91.
3. Thomas L. Haskell, "Capitalism and the Origins of the Humanitarian Sensibility," Part 1, American Historical Review 90 (June 1985):339–61.

Bibliographic Citations

Haskell, Thomas L. "Capitalism and the Origins of the Humanitarian Sensibility," Part 1. American Historical Review 90 (June 1985):339–61.

Headrick, Daniel R. The Tools of Empire: Technology and European Imperialism in the Nineteenth Century. New York: Oxford University Press, 1981.

You should use the form of these endnotes and bibliographical citations as the models for your own citations. Ask your professor if there is a preferred form of citations he or she wants you to use. If not, use these and look through the examples in Chapters 5, 6, and 7 for other models. There are additional examples below. Because there is no standardized form, historical journals and books use slightly different forms. Journals have different editorial guides, so you will see different forms of endnotes in different journals. Many journals use footnotes at the bottom of each page, rather than endnotes at the end of the article. Use endnotes for your paper, unless your teacher instructs you otherwise.

Don't worry. Be accurate and consistent and you will do well. Citations become much easier with practice.

GUIDES TO STYLE

There are many more extensive treatments of documentation techniques. They tend to overwhelm the reader with detail, but they should be turned to for reference. Four helpful reference aids for the mechanics of papers are:

The Chicago Manual of Style. 13th ed. Chicago: University of Chicago Press, 1982.

Turabian, Kate L. *A Manual for Writers of Term Papers, Theses, and Dissertations.* 4th ed. Chicago: University of Chicago Press, 1973.

Barzun, Jacques and Graff, Henry F. *The Modern Researcher.* 4th ed. San Diego: Harcourt Brace Jovanovich, 1985.

Strunk, William Jr. and White, E.B. *The Elements of Style.* 3d. ed. New York: Macmillan Publishing Co., 1979.

ADDITIONAL EXAMPLES OF DOCUMENTATION

We have already seen the proper forms of citation for journal articles and for books. Single authors, multiple authors, editors, and translators have been cited. Here are some more unusual examples of bibliographic citations of sources:

Citation of a quotation from an interview:

Hicks, Perry. Interview by Sam Howie, Marion, N.C. December 31, 1975. Appalachian State University Oral History Program, Appalachian State University, Boone, N.C.

Citation of a book review:

Huttenback, Robert A. Review of Uncertain Dimensions: Western Overseas Empires in the Twentieth Century by Raymond F. Betts in The American Historical Review 91 (April 1986):363-64.

Citation of a newspaper article, with a by-line:

Tedford, Ted. "S. Africa Moving to End Apartheid, Spokesman Says." Free Press Staff Writer. The Burlington Free Press Burlington, Vermont. (June 17, 1986): 1:1.

Citation of a government document:

U.S. Internal Revenue Service, 1981 Statistics of Income: Corporation Income Tax Returns.

Washington, D.C.: U.S. Government Printing Office, 1984.

Citation of an article in an edited book:

Nash, Daphne. "Historical archaeology" in Andrew Sherratt, ed. The Cambridge Encyclopedia of Archaeology. New York: Cambridge University Press, 1980. 43–46.

Citation of two books by the same author:

Tuchman, Barbara W. The Proud Tower: A Portrait of the World Before the War, 1890–1914. New York: Bantam Books, 1962.

---. Distant Mirror: The Calamitous 14th Century. New York: Ballantine Books, 1978.

[8] *A Concise Guide to Usage*

PREVIEW: *In this chapter we present nine rules of effective writing, chosen because they are so often violated by the unwary writer. Read through the chapter to familiarize yourself with the material, then refer to it again as you revise and proofread your work.*

Usage is the name given to matters of correctness or suitability of language — as simple as that. Most of us learn standard usage from parents, friends, teachers, newspapers and books, radio and television. But we all have lapses and weak points that can be distracting to our readers. That is the reason for this section of the *Writer's Guide.* The rules explained below cover the most common questions of usage. Mastering them will not make you one of the world's great prose stylists, but it will help you to write more clearly and without the distractions that errors of usage can cause your reader.

RULE 1. SUBJECT AND VERB MUST AGREE IN NUMBER.

In English, nouns (and pronouns) and verbs are either singular or plural. If the subject noun (or pronoun) is singular, then the verb of the sentence must also be singular.

Ellen (She) [**singular subject**] swims. [**singular verb**]
The girls (They) [**plural subject**] swim. [**plural verb**]

So far, so good. But sentences like those aren't the ones that give writers problems. The difficulty surfaces when you write a sentence like this one:

The value placed on a free press by the two countries differ drastically.

Does that look all right to you? Let's see: the subject is *value*, singular; the verb is *differ*, plural. Subject and verb do not agree. This kind of error is common, especially in speaking, where it is easy to make. You hear the noun nearest to the verb, *countries*, and create a plural verb to match. Of course, *countries* is not the subject; *value* is. The correct sentence reads:

> The value placed on a free press by the two countries differs drastically.

A simple test for complicated sentences is to omit everything but subject and verb, then look and listen:

> The value . . . differs. . . .

Collective nouns name a group or collection: *herd, club, nation, team,* etc. They take a singular verb if unity is stressed or a plural verb if their plurality is emphasized:

> The faculty *is* empowered to revise the curriculum.
>
> but
>
> The faculty *are* divided on the issue of union representation.

RULE 2. A PRONOUN MUST AGREE IN NUMBER WITH ITS ANTECEDENT.

If the antecedent (the noun that the pronoun replaces) is singular, the pronoun must be singular. If the antecedent is plural, the pronoun must be plural:

> Many people [**plural antecedent**] fail to file their [**plural pronoun**] income taxes on time.

This would seem an easy rule to follow, yet mistakes are common. One student's explanation of how to teach windsurfing contained this sentence:

> Let the learner practice until they feel quite comfortable.

Here the subject (*learner*) is singular, but the pronoun (*they*) is plural. One way of correcting this sentence is to make the noun plural:

> Let learners practice until they feel quite comfortable.

This solution avoids the problem of gender introduced by the alternative:

> Let the learner practice until he (she? he or she?) feels quite comfortable.

Another example of lack of agreement comes from a mail-order flier, urging the reader to order soon:

> Our supply of these free gifts — especially those clever little kitchen clocks — are beginning to run low.

The subject is *supply,* not *gifts* or *clocks.* The verb should be singular too — *is,* not *are.*

RULE 3. USE THE CORRECT FORM OF THE PRONOUN.

The common personal pronouns (*I, me, he, him, she, her, it, we, us, you, they, them*) seldom cause much difficulty. Many writers do have problems with the punctuation of two classes of possessive pronouns. **Never use an apostrophe with these forms:**

possessive forms (act as modifiers)

my	*my* pen
your	*your* books
his	*his* belt
her	*her* car
its	*its* clarity
our	*our* house
your	*your* camera
their	*their* papers

substantive forms (act as nouns)

mine	That pen is *mine.*
yours	Which books are *yours?*
his	The brown belt is *his.*
hers	The second car is *hers.*
its	Of the wines tested for clarity, *its* is best.
ours	The yellow house is *ours.*

yours	What kind of camera is *yours?*
theirs	The papers on the desk are *theirs.*

Note: it's is a contraction of *it is.*

RULE 4. DON'T SHIFT VERB TENSES UNNECESSARILY.

Traditionally, writers in some fields use only the past tense of verbs, treating all events and ideas as if they occurred in the past. Writers in other fields may sometimes use the historical present, treating past events as if they were happening now:

> Shakespeare frequently alternates scenes of terror and tragedy with moments of comic relief.

Use whichever tense best suits your needs. Just be consistent: don't shift from past to present to past without a purpose.

RULE 5. PLACE MODIFIERS AS CLOSE AS POSSIBLE TO WORDS MODIFIED.

Writers-in-training are more likely to violate this rule with multi-word modifiers:

> Mangy and flea-bitten, I saw the dog sitting on my front steps.
>
> Our agency rents cars to salespeople of all sizes.
>
> Bouncing off parked cars, he spotted the driverless truck.

The meaning is clarified by placing the modifiers next to the words described:

> I saw the mangy and flea-bitten dog sitting on my front steps.
>
> Our agency rents cars of all sizes to salespeople.
>
> He spotted the driverless truck bouncing off parked cars.

RULE 6. WRITE COMPLETE SENTENCES.

A **sentence** is a group of words that contains a subject and a verb and expresses a complete thought. This is a sentence:

My shoe is tight.

This is not:

Because my shoe is tight.

Why not? What's the difference? Each group of words has a subject, *shoe,* and a verb, *is.* The only difference between the utterances is the addition of the word *because* to the second. The reason that "Because my shoe is tight" is not a sentence is that it doesn't express a complete thought; it cannot function as an independent unit. Read it aloud and you'll see what we mean. The listener (reader) is left dangling — because my shoe is tight *what?*[1]

Ironically, by adding a word, *because,* to the sentence, we've made it less than complete. This kind of word is called a **subordinator.** One kind of subordinator is the **relative pronoun:** *which, that, who, whom, what,* and *whose* are examples. The **subordinating conjunction** is a second kind. Common subordinating conjunctions are *because, after, when, although, as, before, if, unless, until, when, where.* The effect of adding these subordinators to a clause is to make that clause dependent:

"Because my shoe is tight" is an example of one kind of sentence fragment. It doesn't express a complete thought, it cannot stand alone. It must be attached to a complete sentence, like this:

My foot hurts because my shoe is tight.

The sentence above has two **clauses.** Because the first clause, *my foot hurts,* expresses a complete thought and can stand alone, it is called **independent.** Because the second clause does not express a complete thought and cannot stand alone, it is called **dependent.**

A complete sentence, then, must contain an independent clause. It may contain additional elements as well.

complete sentence (independent clause):

Stan stopped smoking recently.

[1]Speech and writing have different requirements. In the following conversation, "because my shoe is tight" may function perfectly well: "Why are you limping?" "Because my shoe is tight."

complete sentence (two independent clauses and coordinating conjunction):

Stan stopped smoking recently, and he feels healthier.

complete sentence (dependent clause and independent clause):

Since Stan stopped smoking recently, he feels healthier.

RULE 7. AVOID COMMA SPLICE AND RUN-ON.

When independent clauses are joined, you must separate them with a comma plus *and, but, or, for, nor,* or *yet;* or with a colon; or with a semicolon. Violations of this rule are the comma splice and the run-on sentence.

wrong	The fluorescent light over the desk in my office isn't working, it hasn't worked since the painters were here. (comma splice)
correct	The fluorescent light over the desk in my office isn't working, and it hasn't worked since the painters were here.
correct	The fluorescent light over the desk in my office isn't working; it hasn't worked since the painters were here.

Note: See Chapter 9 for use of the colon.

RULE 8. DISTINGUISH BETWEEN HOMOPHONES.

Homophones are words pronounced alike but different in spelling and meaning. Using any of them incorrectly marks your writing as less than meticulous. You should master these common ones:

their, there, they're

their is a possessive pronoun:

on their own, their books

there has three common uses:

1. as an adverb meaning *in, at,* or *to that place:*

    She is going to build an addition there.

2. as a noun meaning *that place:*

    We live near there.

3. as a function word to introduce a clause:

    There are only two choices in the matter.

they're is a contraction of *they are:*

    They're my best friends.

to, too, two

to is a preposition meaning *toward, as far as, until, etc.* With a verb, it is a sign of the infinitive:

    The road to Jeffersonville is closed.

    The second shift is from three to eleven.

    The plant manager likes to play squash. (infinitive)

too is an adverb meaning *also, more than enough:*

    The report was late too.

    Too many cooks spoil the broth.

two is the number between one and three, used as an adjective or a pronoun:

    "Two hamburgers, please."

    Only two survived.

than, then

than is a conjunction used in comparisons:

    She is taller than her brother.

then may be an adverb, adjective, or noun related to time:

    I'm going to the meeting too. I'll see you then.

    Since then he hasn't smiled.

RULE 9. AVOID SEXUALLY-BIASED LANGUAGE.

In recent years we have become much more aware of the ways language shapes our thinking. Most people realize that referring to Italians as "wops," for instance, not only demeans them but also makes it difficult for us to perceive Italians as anything but stereotypes.

We don't believe you're likely to practice racial or national stereotyping in your writing. But we along with millions of other Americans do practice another kind of linguistic bias nearly every time we write. We're talking about sexual bias. Let us show you what we mean:

> Pioneers moved West, taking their wives and children with them.

What's wrong with that sentence? What's wrong is the assumption that the pioneers, the builders of our nation, were all males and that women (and children, for that matter) went along for the ride. That is simply not true. It is this kind of bias, perhaps unconscious, perhaps unintentional, that you need to watch for in your writing.

To be honest, avoiding sexist language isn't always easy. Because the English language lacks a singular pronoun that means *he or she,* the writer constantly has to deal with gender choices like these:

> When the shopper wishes to cash a check, she (he?). . . .
>
> Each student should write his (or her?) name at the top.

As a writer, you do have options:

1. Rewrite to use the plural

   > Sprinters warm up by stretching their muscles. Pianists run over scales and chords to limber their fingers.

2. Rewrite to avoid gender pronouns

   > A sprinter warms up by stretching. A pianist runs over scales and chords.

3. Alternate female and male pronouns

   > A sprinter warms up by stretching her muscles. A pianist runs over scales and chords to limber his fingers.

A Final Word

It is impossible in these few pages to anticipate all the questions you might have as you write your papers. Every writer should have a copy of a handbook of usage, such as *The Heath Handbook,* Eleventh edition, by Langdon Elsbree and Gerald P. Mulderig. Buy one and refer to it as you revise your papers. A few minutes spent in this way can make all the difference on the impact of your paper.

[9] *Make Punctuation Work for You*

PREVIEW: *Correctly used, punctuation aids the reader's understanding of your writing. Incorrectly used, punctuation can confuse or misinform. This chapter focuses on the most common uses of each mark of punctuation. Read through the chapter to familiarize yourself with the material, then refer to it again as you revise and proofread your work.*

We use punctuation marks to clarify the meaning of our writing. Some usages are purely conventional: the colon (:) after "Dear Sir" in a business letter, for instance. Others have been established to make meaning clear. Your primary goal in punctuating should always be clarity of expression. Although common sense will often help you select the correct usage, there is no substitute for knowing a few basic rules.

Comma ,

The comma is the most frequently used, and abused, mark of punctuation. Relatively weak as a separator, it is less emphatic than the colon, semicolon, or dash. It indicates the briefest of pauses. Although there are dozens of uses of the comma, we'll look at only the most common.

To separate items in a series:

> The standard personal computer consists of memory, video display, keyboard, disc drive, and printer.

Note: a comma is used before the *and.*

To set off interrupters:

> The party's candidate for governor, Marie Marshall, offered her plan to reduce the deficit. (appositive)

The flight from Chicago, on the other hand, arrived on time. (parenthetical expression)

Note: Interrupters are enclosed by a *pair* of commas.

To set off a long introductory phrase or clause:

In the deep snows at the top of the mountain, they hid a cache of supplies.

If you want to learn to ski the right way, you should take lessons.

To separate independent clauses joined by and, but, or, nor, for, yet:

Matt was interested in the job, but he didn't want to move away from his family.

The purchasing department ordered new furniture, and the office manager had the rooms painted.

To introduce a short quotation:

The librarian told them, "If you have a question, ask someone."

Semicolon ;

The semicolon provides more separation than the comma, less than the period. Its most common use is to separate independent clauses not joined by *and, but, or, nor, for, yet,* when you wish to show close relationship between those clauses. Otherwise, use a period.

The dean wanted a new curriculum; the faculty did not.
My mother was understanding the first time; she was upset the second time; the third time she was furious.

To Review: To show the degree of relationship between independent clauses, you have three options: comma with coordinating conjunction (*and, but, or, nor, for, yet*), semicolon, and period.

The legislature has been meeting since January, yet they have not passed a single bill.

The legislature has been meeting since January; they have not passed a single bill.

The legislature has been meeting since January. They have not passed a single bill.

Colon :

The colon is used primarily to introduce a word, phrase, or clause that fulfills or explains an idea in the first part of the sentence. It is also used after the salutation of a business letter, to introduce a list, and to separate the title and subtitle of a book. Because it is a strong mark of punctuation, use it only as directed.

To introduce or fulfill:

In that respect, Canada is like the United States: both have large numbers of non-English speakers.

On his deathbed the old miser made only one request: that his gold be buried with him.

To introduce a list:

The demographic study focussed on three factors: population, income, and age.

Note: Do not use a colon directly after a verb.

wrong	On her trip to France she visited: Paris, Chartres, and Mont St. Michel.
correct	On her trip to France she visited Paris, Chartres, and Mont St. Michel.

After the salutation of a business letter:

Dear Mrs. Irving:

To separate the title and the subtitle of a book:

The Golden Bough: A Study in Magic and Religion

Apostrophe ’

The apostrophe has three distinct uses: to mark the omission of one or more letters or numerals, to mark the possessive case, and to mark certain plurals.

To mark the omission of a letter or letters:

wouldn’t	(would not)
can’t	(cannot)
you’ll	(you will)
I’m	(I am)
it’s	(it is)
they’re	(they are)

To mark the omission of one or more numerals:

a ’57 Chevy	a 1957 Chevy
the summer of ’42	the summer of 1942

To form the possessive of a singular or plural noun not ending in s:

girl	girl’s
laboratory	laboratory’s
men	men’s
children	children’s

To form the possessive of a plural noun ending in s:

girls	girls’
books	books’
laboratories	laboratories’

To form the possessive of a singular noun of one syllable ending in s *or* s *sound:*

William James	William James’s philosophy
Brahms	Brahms’s First Symphony

To form the possessive of a singular noun of more than one syllable ending in s *or* s *sound:*

Socrates	Socrates’ school

Note: Do not use an apostrophe with possessive pronouns: *his, hers, yours, ours, theirs, whose, its* (*it's* means *it is*)

Parentheses ( )

Parentheses are used to enclose explanatory material within a sentence when such material is incidental to the main thought. Commas may also be used for this purpose; they are less formal and indicate a closer relationship to the main sentence than parentheses. Some writers use parentheses for the same purpose.

> Senator Arndt (who just happens to be my brother-in-law) wrote the new farm credit bill.
>
> Of his many novels (he wrote more than thirty), *Stairway to Darkness* was his favorite.

Note: Parentheses have special uses in citations. See the section on documentation.

Brackets [ ]

Brackets are marks of punctuation with limited but specific uses, especially in academic writing. Often when you excerpt part of a longer quotation, the meaning is not entirely clear. You may add clarification in brackets.

> "The President [Truman] was determined that war policy be made by civilians, not generals."
>
> "Freud's division of the psyche [id, ego, superego] has been disputed by many in recent years."

When you wish to acknowledge without changing an error in the quoted material, enclose the Latin word *sic* (thus) in brackets:

> "The carriage careened wildly through muddy ruts until it broke an axel [sic]."

Note: Many typewriters do not have brackets. You can ink them in by hand. Do not use parentheses instead of brackets.

Ellipsis . . .

The omission (ellipsis) of part of a quoted passage is indicated by ellipsis marks: three spaced periods. Use these marks when you are quoting a long passage but wish to omit material.

> "These matriarchal tribes . . . often fight small wars to extend their territory."

When you delete the end of a sentence, use four periods:

> "Four score and seven years ago our fathers brought forth on this continent, a new nation. . . . Now we are engaged in a great civil war, testing whether that nation, or any nation so conceived and so dedicated, can long endure."

Dash —

The dash is probably the most overused mark of punctuation. Because it is so emphatic, its misuse stands out glaringly and is viewed as the sign of an overemotional style. Employ the dash only as described below.

To show an abrupt break in thought:

> I explained all that to you yesterday when — oh, but that wasn't you.

To introduce a word or words for emphasis:

> You have only one choice — do it!

To separate a final summarizing clause from the preceding idea:

> Food, clothing, shelter, and fuel — these are all that Thoreau claimed are needed to sustain life.

Note: To type a dash, use two hyphens (--). Do not leave a space before or after the hyphens.

Quotation Marks " "

Quotation marks enclose the precise words spoken or written by someone other than the writer. Do not use them to identify indirect quotations or summaries.

To enclose direct quotations:

> In his book Bronsky asserts, “Mussolini's leadership was not entirely bad for Italy.”
>
> Franklin Delano Roosevelt's powerful words, “The only thing we have to fear is fear itself,” were spoken in the depths of national depression.

Note: When the quoted passage is embedded in a sentence, it is preceded by a comma (and followed by one if the sentence continues beyond the quotation).

Exception: Long quotations (more than four typed lines) are indented ten spaces and double spaced. Quotation marks are not used.

A quotation within a quotation uses single marks within double marks:

> In his inaugural speech Governor Harris urged her listeners to “Remember President Kennedy's message ‘Ask not what your country can do for you — ask what you can do for your country.’”

Note: Periods and commas are placed inside the quotation marks. Semicolons and colons are placed outside. Question marks, exclamation points, and dashes are placed outside the quotation marks unless they are part of the original quotation.

To mark the titles of short stories, poems, essays, articles, and chapters of books, songs, symphonies, and plays in collections:

> Hemingway's story “The Snows of Kilimanjaro”
>
> Shelley's poem “To a Skylark”

Note: When they appear in the text, titles of books, full-length plays, magazines, and newspapers are *italicized* or *underlined,* not placed in quotation marks.

Further Thoughts on Reading and Writing History

At the end of the process of writing this book, we find ourselves still thinking about how we learn through the interaction of reading and writing. We recognize that we are altered as readers and writers of history as a result of examining what we do.

While writing *Writer's Guide: History,* we discovered and explored what it is we ask our students to do when they read and write history in the courses we teach. Acting as historians, we imaginatively placed ourselves into the context of student writing and learning. We remembered ourselves as students in this renewed awareness of how we have continued to learn through reading, writing, and sharing knowledge with students and colleagues.

Through this particular act of writing as learning, we reaffirmed our belief that "doing history" requires our full activity and attention, our greatest imaginative powers of writing and thinking. Writing about writing history — as well as writing history — taps long-term memory as source of remembered experience and short-term memory for immediate information. Although finishing a piece of writing that others will read and appreciate brings its own rewards, much of our delight comes from what we have learned about the rich interplay between writing and learning history. It's as if we've taken on some of what it is to be students again through identifying with what students of history do. Once more, we've expanded our range of experience in history.

But just as anyone who reads and writes history comes to understand that there are no simple accounts of human actions, no simple causal explanations for human events, so have we come to recognize that the simplest acts of reading and writing are embedded in a complex of background events, beliefs, language structures, attitudes, and behaviors. After our work on *Writer's Guide: History,* we cannot return to our old assumptions about reading and writing history as writers, as teachers, or as historians.

Index

1 2 3 4 5 6 7 8 9 10